This book is, quite simply, a valuable read for believers, non-believers, and everyone in between. Drew Cordell plainly has a powerful mind, deep research capability, and a careful ear for the questions that people ask and need answers to.

I have found it to be very informative and easy to read, and I sincerely commend it. Our world has been shaped by religious ideas, both good and bad. As an attempt to make sense of it all, there is much of real value in these pages.

THE HON JOHN ANDERSON AC FTSE
Former Deputy Prime Minister of Australia

Drew has packed this one book with more wisdom and grace than most apologists have done. What sets it apart is its deeply personal and humble approach, in stark contrast to the heroic and triumphant tone often found in similar works—the former style I find much more appealing. Rather than inundating readers with an overwhelming deluge of data and scientific arguments, Drew strikes a delicate balance, avoiding naivety while remaining approachable.

One of the book's notable strengths is its reliance on reasonable evidence, eschewing the sole reliance on biblical quotations that we see all too frequently in other similar books. This approach not only informs but also respects non-Christian readers, creating a space for dialogue and understanding.

You need not wholeheartedly agree with all the book's assertions before recommending it to a friend. The book sets up conversations for you to follow up, and different views to tease open. This is the book's major strength in my view. No more passing out of gospel tracts within a set-and-forget type evangelistic mode. This text will help you to maintain an ongoing dialogue.

Lastly, the text operates on two fundamental assumptions. Firstly, it assumes that orthodox historic Christianity can stand firmly when articulated clearly, which Drew does without apology. However, for many Christians who may not subscribe to these beliefs intellectually and rely on alternative cultural viewpoints, the book may challenge them to present equally lucid explanations. Secondly, and notably, the text presupposes that non-Christian readers ideally possess a solid familiarity with the life and teachings of Jesus before delving into its pages. For those whose knowledge is primarily gleaned from movies and memes, the book may remain enigmatic.

REV DR IAN ROBINSON
Former Alan Walker Lecturer in Leadership, Evangelism, Apologetics and Mission, United Theological College. Author of *This Thirsty Heart: A Journey in the Heart of Australia*, Creator of the *Makes You Wonder* course. Oxford University: MA Theology, Charles Sturt University: PhD, Doctor of Philosophy, Desert Spirituality.

While this book hasn't altered my worldview, I did find it helpful to better understand the origins of the Christian faith and the available evidence that enables some to believe in the Christian message.

RHETT
Agnostic

This is a straightforward and sympathetic attempt to clear the ground for people who want to explore faith. Drew is obviously familiar with the sorts of arguments that the thinking non-Christian makes. His approach is honest and undefensive and this should help people with real questions who want to know what the true foundations are.

As the leader of an inclusive evangelical church, I can't endorse his traditional position on homosexuality but that does not mean I can't appreciate the apologetic work he has produced in this book.

JOHN PETERS
Rector of St Mary's Bryanston Square London. Author of *Third Person: The Work of the Holy Spirit* and *Message: Send: Communicating the Gospel in a Post-Truth Culture*. Creator of *The Life Course*. Oxford University: Bachelor of Theology and Law.

Drew has brought together an accessible and friendly set of responses to some of the questions that reflective people sometimes raise about the Christian faith. He writes personally and honestly, recognizing areas of mystery, misunderstanding, and disagreement, and engaging readers with his own thoughtfully held convictions. For those exploring faith, this straightforward and thorough book could be an excellent resource.

JENNY DAWKINS
Formerly Associate Vicar of All Saints Peckham. University of Cambridge: Bachelor of Theology. Kings College London: MA Biblical Studies.

Honest Christianity addresses issues that non-believers and skeptics find interesting and relevant. As a popular-level book, the average reader will be able to understand the content and be challenged to consider the truth of Christianity. Any serious skeptic or interested Christian should find something challenging about this book as well as relevant sources to enhance their study.

DR J. BRIAN HUFFLING
Director of the Ph.D. Program and Associate Professor of Philosophy and Theology: Southern Evangelical Seminary. BA History: Lee University. MA Apologetics, Biblical Studies, Philosophy: Southern Evangelical Seminary. PhD Philosophy of Religion: Southern Evangelical Seminary.

This book helpfully engages with many of life's most difficult questions. Drew Cordell has undertaken rigorous research on numerous topics, and he presents it in an accessible way. He helps distinguish fact from fiction, enabling readers to make informed decisions about issues that really matter.

RUTH JACKSON
Producer and Presenter for the Unbelievable? Apologetics podcast.
Oxford University: MA Theology.

This honest and engaging book is a valuable resource for anyone who wants to seriously engage the question of whether the claims of Christianity are true. Drew tackles important issues, does not avoid potentially embarrassing passages of Scripture, gives reasonable answers and evidence, and does so in an accessible format rather than a lengthy academic tome. The section on the development of the canon of Scripture is alone worth the price, explaining the historical process in detail, and allowing questions of legitimacy to be seriously considered. This book will be an excellent aid in producing quality conversations about faith.

DR DARRELL DOOYEMA
Colorado Christian University. MA Philosophy: Denver Seminary. DMin Philosophy, Theology, & Culture: Talbot School of Theology.

This book is both intelligent and witty. Drew's personality and humor shine through, which makes for a pleasant read.

Drew's takes a look both inside and outside the Bible for valuable information, giving a full and well-rounded read. He does a deep dive into the context of scripture and the cultural understanding of the time. We see him mapping-out biblical landscapes, using current and relevant analogies to help us understand what is being communicated. Furthermore, he illuminates the culture and the unique situations faced by people in biblical societies with great descriptive detail.

This book is both enlightening and rich with information. Drew answers some tough questions in a helpful and down-to-earth way.

It is written with humility and honesty, and whether you agree with his opinion or stance on specific issues discussed, you'll see Drew's courage and bravery in naming his personal stance and conviction. He offers clarity on matters that might appear ambiguous to others, avoiding the temptation to merely utilize the 'Both-And' approach often employed to navigate tricky questions.

I'm sure the reader will come away enriched and challenged in a good way.

REV PAUL SAWREY
Middlesex University: BA Hons Theology

In this book, Drew Cordell addresses many potential obstacles to Christian belief. One of the book's key strengths stems from Drew's willingness to face disconcerting issues and potentially awkward passages of scripture. In each instance, key issues and questions are set out and relevant evidence is brought to bear on them. Furthermore, this evidence is presented in a readable and accessible way, employing illustrations where needed and using nontechnical language throughout. For anyone, including both Christians and non-Christians, wanting to wrestle with the question of whether Christianity's truth claims just might be true and worthy of belief, this book will be a helpful resource.

DR PAUL CHAMBERLAIN
Professor, Philosophy of Religion, Ethics & Leadership: Trinity Western University.
Author of *Why People Don't Believe* and *Can We Be Good Without God?*

HONEST CHRIS†IANITY

Why People Still Choose to Believe

DREW CORDELL

HONEST
CHRIS†IANITY
MEDIA

Copyright © 2024 by Drew Cordell

All rights reserved. No part of this book may be reproduced or used in any manner without written permission of the copyright owner except for the use of quotations in a book review. For more information email drew@honestchristianity.org.

First paperback edition March 2024

Cover and interior design by Julie Karen Hodgins

Scriptures taken from the Holy Bible, New International Version®, NIV®. Copyright © 1973, 1978, 1984, 2011 by Biblica, Inc.™ Used by permission of Zondervan. All rights reserved worldwide. www.zondervan.com. The "NIV" and "New International Version" are trademarks registered in the United States Patent and Trademark Office by Biblica, Inc.™

ISBN: 978-0-6458365-0-9 (paperback)
ISBN: 978-0-6458365-1-6 (ebook)

www.honestchristianity.org

Dedicated to all those people
who have taught me to ask the hard questions
and dig deep for the answers.

CONTENTS

Acknowledgements	*xi*
Preface	*xiii*
Chapter 1: Did God Create?	1
Chapter 2: If God Is Our Creator, Why Is There Suffering?	5
Chapter 3: Should We Take the Bible Seriously?	9
Chapter 4: Did Jesus Exist? Who Was He?	67
Chapter 5: Jesus Is Famous Because...	75
Chapter 6: What Do the Miracles Mean?	81
Chapter 7: Does Objective Morality Exist?	101
Chapter 8: Is God a Genocidal Maniac?	107
Chapter 9: Is God a Promoter of Slavery?	111
Chapter 10: Is God a Misogynist?	121
Chapter 11: Is God a Homophobe?	137
Chapter 12: What About the Crusades and Other Atrocities?	141
Chapter 13: What About Other Religions?	149
Chapter 14: If I Refuse Am I Going to Hell?	157
Chapter 15: Where to from Here?	165
Appendices	*169*
Endnotes	*191*
List of Images and Illustrations	*217*
List of Tables	*219*

ACKNOWLEDGEMENTS

A book as personal as this has many contributors who have crossed paths with me in my lifetime. Initial thanks to my mother and father who have loved me, served me, and embodied the very character of Jesus in all their actions.

To my precious wife, who chooses to see the best in me and disregard the worst. To my darling boys, who keep me young and energized.

Nothing is completely original, so thanks to all the scholars who did the hard yards I benefited from in writing this book. Thanks to Phil Baker and John Peters who modelled how to communicate Christian truths dynamically to a non-Christian audience.

Thanks to Rhett, Brenton, Charlotte, and Adam who were key early readers of the first draft. They certainly helped to make it better. Thanks to Hans who helped me navigate the realm of biblical archaeology—not an easy area.

Thank you to Pete and Gillie who have been a constant source of encouragement to my wife and me.

Thank you to my editor Kristen who removed my Aussie slang and made this book better. James has financially helped me with the production of this book. Thank you, James, for the support.

An author is only as good as their book designer, and I'm thankful I found Julie. Thank you Julie for all the hard work and devotion in creating this book with me.

And at risk of sounding like an Oscars speech, I'd like to thank God for enabling someone like me to play a part in revealing truth to the world.

PREFACE

It's early on a Tuesday morning, and I'm driving my usual route into work. This is a regularly trodden path, a road I am all too familiar with. On the left side of the road, I spot a bright-colored, somewhat hipster banner labeled "Free Coffee Wed 10 a.m. to 12 p.m." As I drive closer, I see that the banner is set against the backdrop of a church. The building is probably from the 1970s, which is rather young in terms of the global church, but in Australian terms, we could semi-seriously call this building ancient history. The church certainly looks unchanged since the seventies—somewhat tired. I can't help but ponder whether its appearance is indicative of its overall organizational health. Got a pulse, but only just. Surely this $350 banner is just a hopeless exercise. The act of a probably-gray-haired church committee to say that they "tried something" to engage the local community, though in reality they know deep down that nothing will cut through to a disinterested and otherwise occupied modern society.

I imagine that this experience from my daily commute is similar to the view that the majority of the Western world holds of the Christian church. Churches occupy prime real estate with historical relics, and we just drive past them, ignore them, and wait for the inevitable Starbucks and twenty-four-hour gym/hipster apartment combo to show up. Sure, a charitable arm might say that the church had some relevance and contribution to make years ago, but we've all moved on, haven't we?

As a Christian and member of a church community, I have arrived at the conclusion that we, "the church," in the Western world have failed. I know that some Christian leaders will rail with indignation as they read this, but to do so is simply to bury one's head in the sand. It doesn't matter which metric one chooses to examine, they all tell the same story. Generation after generation is leaving the church and the Christian faith in droves. If you profess to be a Christian then you cannot observe what is happening and ignore it or make excuses. One needs to pause, analyze, and—most importantly—do something to alter the trajectory.

This book is my attempt to do something. For many years I have entered into countless discussions and debates regarding the meaning of our universe over red wine and all other manner of gastronomic goodness with people from all backgrounds. I have found that making the case for the Christian worldview is quite a time-consuming exercise, and as I've grown older, I've realized that is probably a necessary thing. The Christian worldview claims to answer life's most difficult questions. Therefore, it shouldn't come as a surprise that you cannot answer all these questions between the entrée and the cheese board.

Often at these social gatherings I've been asked for an additional resource that one might peruse if they wanted to know more about the Christian message. I have never been completely confident in referring anyone to a "wholistic" resource that can do such a thing in an effective way. Thus, I have written this book.

It has also been my experience that a lot of people really want to believe the Christian message. They see its appeals, benefits, and even sometimes, rationality. However, at the end of the day they just want to know whether its claims are true and trustworthy. As C. S. Lewis most famously said, "Christianity, if false, is of no importance, and if true, of infinite importance. The one thing it cannot be is moderately important."[1]

If you read this book, then at best you may discover that the Christian message is the way, the truth, and the life. At worst you will have spent approximately seven hours and thirty-seven minutes investigating the claims of the most famous person that has ever walked planet earth. Either way, the time would have been well spent given the significant influence that Christianity has played in the world.

As this book is setting out a case for why people choose to be "Christian," it would be helpful at the outset to clarify what a Christian fundamentally is. In today's world there are multiple understandings of what it means to be a Christian. In my experience, some define Christianity as being white and middle class. Others define it as an inherited product, having grown up with

Christian parents. In some parts of the world, it can come down to whether you vote Republican or Democrat.

Allow me to clarify. Your race or ethnic background does not define whether you are a Christian. Your parentage and what their respective religious identification is or was does not define whether you are a Christian. Your church attendance or lack thereof does not define whether you are a Christian. Whether you are a good person or not likewise does not finalize the matter.

Let me broadly identify in a succinct manner what the great majority of Christians believe a Christian to be.

A Christian is someone who believes the following:

1. God created the universe and everything in it.
2. God created human beings with a capacity to relate to him, as distinct from other creatures.
3. As human beings, we consistently fall short of the best that God intends for us and our world, which creates a gap between us and God.
4. Through belief in the death and resurrection of Jesus Christ, we can bridge this gap to God once and for all.
5. God then wants to be intimately involved in our lives, helping you and I to bring about a better world where justice, peace, and prosperity reign for all.

You may have noted that being a Christian is not fundamentally based upon how often you go to church, whether you kneel at an altar, what you eat, etc. It is centered around some biggish ideas, which future chapters in this book will unpack further.

I am fully aware of how big and bold many of the aforementioned claims are, but I believe that these claims can be intelligently evidenced and argued for. Now, when I say that they can be intelligently evidenced, I'm not going to justify any of the above using the religious text of the Bible alone. I've seen many a "teacher" do this, and if you have too, I very much empathize with your frustration. While I believe that the Bible does help us understand these claims, there is a broader vein of evidence that we can draw upon—one that gives the Christian faith so much color, vitality, and sophistication.

At this early point I would encourage you to take ten minutes, write down the above claims, and makes notes against each. Do you believe that a god or gods created the universe, and if so, why? Conversely, if you believe that a creator god or gods is unlikely, why? Once you've made these notes, put them to one side. After you've made it through all these chapters, reflect on what you think to be true in light of what I've written.

I appreciate that many of you perhaps have not had positive interactions with people who claim to be Christians. In terms of branding, Christians struggle. In my experience, current-day Christians tend to live in an echo chamber and struggle to connect with people who are outside this Christian bubble. It can be quite infuriating.

Despite the encounters that you and I may have had with the Christian bubble, those experiences are just that: experiences. While it's inevitable that we will draw some conclusions about religious groups based on these experiences, we need to be careful not to be too firm in our judgments based on these interactions alone. It then becomes something of a task to get rid of all the noise, get rid of our misconceptions, and get to the crux (pardon the pun) of what it really means to be a Christian.

There is one more clarification that I would like to make right up front. If you're exploring the Christian faith primarily because you want your life to be materially better, happier, and easier, then the Christian message might severely disappoint you. This is not a self-help book. As you read on, you will see that I think the Christian faith is true and the best explanation and arranger for many of the most important pillars of life.

Please don't hear me wrong here. I'm not suggesting that to be a Christian is to depart on a self-destructing pilgrimage. That's too far the other way. I'm simply making the point that if you're channeling Janis Joplin and wishing that God would buy you a Mercedes-Benz, that is probably not going to be his top priority should you decide to follow him. His top priority is to ensure that your life contains the fullest purpose, spice, and meaning. For this, Christianity has something to say.

I sincerely hope you enjoy the book. Happy investigating.

Drew

CHAPTER 1

DID GOD CREATE?

If one is to make a case for Christianity, then it is wise to start exploring this very foundational question at the outset. Of all the debates around life's meaning, the question of the universe's origin is definitely the most well-trodden area. YouTube is filled with debates and countless sound bites from scientists and other thinkers, and the literary landscape has a wealth of insight in this area too.

This is a debate that I used to engage in fairly regularly, but as I'm getting older (and hopefully wiser), I find it a little tiring. It seems to me that we now have two very well-carved-out sides, which both overreach in their conclusions given the evidence we have at our disposal.

I have concluded that the discipline of science has neither proven nor disproven the existence of God. However, it's difficult to argue against the proposition that the intellectual bent of scientists moves more favorably towards God's non-existence rather than his existence. I think this is primarily due to the following predominant views:

1. You cannot be a scientist and believe in miracles.
2. To believe in God is to believe in the literal interpretation of Genesis 1–2 in the Bible, which contradicts the current scientific evidence.

You Cannot Be a Scientist and Believe in Miracles

This point doesn't really need any further explanation, does it? Miracles don't and cannot occur. The Bible is full of weird claims, and not all of them can be passed off as allegorical stories. The question of Jesus's supposed death and resurrection is not up for debate in terms of its propositional basis. The gospel writings and other subsequent accounts strongly claim that Jesus physically died and physically rose again. There is no dodging the claim.

To be a Christian is to believe this very thing. If you do believe this occurred and you don't feel stupid or exposed in its articulation (at least some of the time), then I think it's fair to say that you probably haven't critically examined whether this miracle really occurred. There are two certainties in life, as we all know: death and taxes. But really, taxes is added for comedic value. There is only one true certainty in all existence, and it is death for us all.

So when a person claims that someone has violated the most certain rule in the observable universe, your first and most rational response would be to conclude that such a violation did not take place. It is far more reasonable to presume that there is an alternative explanation for why such an event may have been perceived. Think of the re-entering space junk that is commonly mistaken for a UFO.

People have tried to find the "space junk explanation" for the supposed resurrection of Jesus, but it just hasn't been found. In my opinion no one can sufficiently explain why Jesus became the most famous person of all time without the resurrection. This makes Jesus the most awkward and tricky character in the history of the world for scientists and historians alike.

One can obviously still conclude (and many do) that miracles don't happen and the resurrection of Jesus didn't take place. But to do so is to create another unresolved miracle: the miracle of Jesus becoming the most famous person of all time. The key question of debate then becomes which miracle is easier to accept. Rarely do I see scientists, especially in the new-atheist realm, acknowledge the weight of the anthropological evidence that I've just alluded to. I think to not do so is to be quite biased and narrow in thought. Or, in other words, somewhat unscientific.

Therefore, to reject the resurrection on the scientific basis that miracles don't occur produces a somewhat self-defeating outcome. That being the inevitable acceptance of Jesus's unexplained fame and influence. It doesn't seem to matter which side one chooses. At the end of the day, we are all somewhat comfortable accepting that events have occurred without a full and articulated explanation.

At this juncture, with two miracles to consider, I think the most prudent and scientific approach is to ascertain which miracle carries the greatest probability of reflecting the truth of the matter. This should involve delving into historical method and investigating the multiple theories that have been put forward to, if possible, arrive at a conclusion.

To Believe in God Is to Believe in the Literal Interpretation of Genesis 1–2 in the Bible

Thankfully, this area has been addressed very well by many scholars over the past few decades, but I have seen the occasional flutter of debate in this area, so I will quickly address it here.

The broad headline is this: The great majority of serious Christian thinkers and biblical scholars conclude that you can affirm the theory of evolution and believe that the creation account in Genesis carries integrity at the same time. How?

Well, in all likelihood the Genesis account of creation is not a literal explanation of how the universe came into being. The Genesis account parallels the framework of other creation accounts that are documented in the ancient world.[1] These accounts are all polytheistic and predominantly hold the sun, moon, and stars as deities. In addition, these competing accounts state that mankind was created to be a slave of the gods. According to the Babylonian epic the *Enuma Elish*, one group of gods rebelled against another and was then defeated. The defeated group was imprisoned as punishment and forced to act as servants of the victors. However, Marduk, one of the victorious gods, decided to relieve the imprisoned gods of these duties and created mankind instead to become servants to the victorious gods. To make this happen, the ringleader of the rebels, Kingu, was killed and his blood was used to create mankind.

A similar rationale for the creation of mankind is also found in the Atrahasis epic.[2]

The Genesis account is different. First, it is monotheistic. Where the sun, moon, and stars are deities in the other accounts, in Genesis, they are created by the one God. Men and women are created not to be slaves but as free beings with major responsibilities over the created order, which God gave to them to enjoy and curate.[3]

In my opinion, it is more likely that the Genesis account of creation was written to address the aforementioned ancient worldviews of the time and was not a literal scientific explanation of the origins of the universe and mankind. Its primary focus is on communicating theological truths about the world in a largely symbolic, pictorial literary style.[4] To read it as a science textbook seems to be a strange interpretive move completely out of step with common sense.

Returning to the Original Question

Ultimately, you can still be a scientist, a proponent of rational thought, and be open to the idea that a creator God exists. As I've said earlier, no one can prove that a creator God exists. No serious Christian thinker is asking that you would move to such a firm conclusion on the basis of scientific evidence. However, I think it reasonable to remain open to the idea of a creator God; you don't have to be a crazy irrational fool to do so.

CHAPTER 2

IF GOD IS OUR CREATOR, WHY IS THERE SUFFERING?

In the previous chapter I made the case that one can be open to the idea that God created the universe and not necessarily be unscientific at the same time. If that's the case, then seemingly God created a universe that delivers tremendous suffering and pain. If this potential God is worth exploring further, then I must also seek to understand how it is in anyone's interests to allow the Boxing Day Tsunami of 2004 to take place, which claimed in excess of 230,000 lives.[1] If we suggest that the earth is created by a supreme being who is supposedly good, how could he allow such an atrocity to take place?

I, like many of you, am seriously troubled by this question. All of us who care about our planet and fellow humanity should be. I don't think it's a question that you can simply square off once and for all. It is always there, always demanding thought and response.

In some periods of my life, I have occasionally leaned towards thinking that God doesn't exist. How could he? If he does, surely he wouldn't allow such crap to take place. The hypothesis then becomes: Gratuitous evil and suffering exists; therefore, God doesn't exist.

Before we test this hypothesis, we need to first examine its underlying premise: The existence of gratuitous evil and suffering precludes God's existence.

In moments of pain, I have often thought that if God existed, he would be good and caring. He surely wouldn't allow such seemingly meaningless atrocities to take place—whether in my life or the lives of other people. To be honest, I'm not really sure why I think this. I can't say that it's based on any empirical evidence or philosophical reasoning, it just hangs in my gut and feels instinctive. Rather than rely on my gut, however, I should drill a bit deeper into this, which leads me to ask: How confident am I that God's existence hinges on an absolute zero level of gratuitous suffering and evil in our world?

Depending on my mood, my confidence level ranges from 95 percent right through to 10 percent. I remember in 2014 watching a BBC documentary that explored the rule of the Libyan ruler Muammar Gaddafi.[2] At the end of the program, I remember feeling sad and hopeless, and I sensed the utter absence of God in the victims' lives who suffered at the hand of this truly vicious and evil tyrant. Surely these victims wouldn't entertain the idea of a god—not a loving one anyway. At that moment I think I would have been about 95 percent confident on my scale, with the needle really flexing toward 100. However, I have never found myself feeling 100 percent confident that the existence of gratuitous suffering precludes a god from existing. Given this, I am compelled to consider the following: God may exist in a world where gratuitous suffering and evil are present.

There are a few roads one can take in response to this hypothesis. The first being:

1. Get angry

This is a common position held by higher profile atheists in recent history, including Christopher Hitchens, Stephen Fry, and Richard Dawkins.

Steven Fry, in his somewhat famous 2015 interview with Gay Byrne, outlined a response that received much publicity.[3] In it he discussed several instances of suffering, which demonstrated that God was (in his words) "monstrous, utterly monstrous, and he deserves no respect whatsoever."

He also stated that God "could easily have made a creation in which [suffering] didn't exist."

That last quote is very important as it is this premise—that God really could have done things differently—that Fry has based his entire grievance upon. When one really pauses to reflect upon it, it is an extraordinary statement, said so confidently by Fry. How can he be confident that God could have done things differently? In my years of study and thought, I have never found a compelling response to this question.

In addition, I would challenge whether Fry's angry response to God is a realistic and well-thought-through human response to such a revelation. That revelation being:

1. God, you do exist.
2. You're seemingly a more powerful being than I.
3. You've created the universe, including me.

At this juncture is Fry really going to tell God that he is doing a bad job? I'm not sure he is. What about his Cambridge education? Stellar acting career, fame, money, opportunities? Can any of that get a mention?

In summary, I do in part empathize with Fry's response, but I consider it to be very unbalanced and somewhat disingenuous. He cherry-picks the worst of life while not giving due consideration to the better stuff in our world and beyond.

A second possible response to the hypothesis mentioned previously is to:

2. Be apathetic

As mentioned earlier, this is a question that one cannot simply square off once and for all. As such, one could argue that any effort expelled searching for an answer is futile. I don't personally feel that this is a good approach; while a final definitive answer seems unlikely, this doesn't mean philosophical value can't be extracted through the process of searching.

A third possible response is to:

3. Dig deeper

I think it worthwhile at this point is to ask oneself the following question: Do I see enough good in this so-called God to warrant my continued interest and investigation in him, despite all the suffering that I see in the world?

If God did create this world and everything in it, what are the good things about it? Are there good things in my life that I could potentially attribute to him? Are there instances through the history of the world where God's goodwill has been tangibly demonstrated to humankind? I feel that these questions are the most productive way forward to address the challenge of suffering and evil in our lives and in the broader world.

In summary, I do not believe the existence of gratuitous suffering and evil precludes the existence of God. I have not seen a conclusive argument made for this assertion.

All that said, I can appreciate that many of you will find this intellectual toing and froing all rather unsatisfactory. Maybe life has been or is very tough at the minute and the last thing you need is someone intellectualizing why God might in fact be tacitly permissive in the challenges you're currently encountering. I do understand that.

At this point I really want to encourage you to not throw in the towel with God just yet. I wish I had a more conclusive response to the question of suffering, but I don't believe that we as humans can obtain this in our lifetime. I don't believe that permanently dismissing God out of anger helps any of us move forward.

CHAPTER 3

SHOULD WE TAKE THE BIBLE SERIOUSLY?

In the previous chapter I discussed the question of suffering and how it relates to God's supposed existence. I suggested that the existence of suffering, rather than disproving God, should actually prompt us to make further inquiry into the character of God. Is God a monster? Is God loving? Is God generous? Is God interested in the world? Is God a racist? Is God sexist? Does God care at all about my life and how I live it?

The Christian faith claims that we already have a very solid indication of what God's character is because it has been revealed to us through history in a book called the Bible.

Now, a bit of a warning. This chapter is by far the longest in this book—significantly longer than the others. The reason is that without establishing the credibility of the Bible, we might as well throw all the other chapters in the trash. The chapter has been segmented into five subheadings (outlined below) which will make it easier to digest. With that said, let's launch into it.

The Bible is not actually one singular book but a collection of books. The first part is called the Old Testament, and it is comprised of thirty-nine books; the second part is called the New Testament, and it is comprised of twenty-seven books. In total, the Bible has more than forty different authors and was written over a 1,600-year period.[1]

All of this means that the Bible is a very complex document that needs thorough study, consideration, and reflection. Too often when I enter into discussions with people about the Bible (including Christians and non-religious people), it becomes apparent that they have firm opinions on its meaning in a whole variety of areas but have not actually conducted a proper inquiry into the wide variety of scholarship and diversity of opinion that is available today.

I think one of the main reasons Western society is quick to make snap judgments on the Bible is that we now approach literature in a very consumerist manner. We are living in a digital world where nearly anyone across the planet can communicate with anyone else at a moment's notice. As such communication passes and evaporates on a rapid scale, and we are conditioned to interpret data quickly—otherwise we will never get anything done. If you are like me, you never read a quarter of your emails and your eyes are a constant filter, prioritizing those communications that you need to see and disregarding those you don't. I don't think this mindset bodes well for Bible interpretation, and I see many people make quick and erroneous judgments regarding the Bible's meaning without letting it intellectually marinate.

With all that said, why do some people take such an ancient collection of texts so seriously? Well, I think we should for the following reasons:

i. **Archaeological Evidence:** Archaeological findings to date suggest that the Bible may indeed be communicating history.
ii. **Manuscript Transmission:** We can be confident that the Bible in our possession today is very close in wording to the original manuscripts.
iii. **Historical Credibility:** The accounts of Jesus's life and resurrection were written sufficiently close enough to the events to lend them historical credibility.
iv. **Undiluted Motives:** There is no serious evidence to suggest that any of the biblical writings were engineered by authority figures to exercise control.
v. **Still Relevant Today:** The Bible makes some startling claims regarding the meaning and function of the universe that, if true, change the way we see everything.

i. Archaeological Evidence
Archaeological Findings to Date Suggest That the Bible May Indeed Be Communicating History

On one hand, many archaeologists and historians are quite comfortable accepting that the Bible in all likelihood is communicating significant portions of history. On the other hand, however, it purports the existence of miracles, which is just plain silly. As such, the Bible rests in very uncomfortable territory within the scholarly realm. In this first section, I'll outline a "greatest hits" list of archaeological evidence for the Bible, which causes it to occupy such a unique and contested position within scholarship.

Old Testament

Exodus

Many of you have heard of or seen one of the very first Hollywood blockbusters: *The Ten Commandments*, which was made way back in 1956. In this movie, the Bible story of the Exodus is portrayed, which involves the Hebrew leader Moses guiding his fellow Hebrews out of Egyptian slavery under the reign of Pharaoh Ramses II. It's an epic tale that contains several miraculous phenomena, ranging from an epic frog plague to a dramatic escape from Egypt through the parting of the Red Sea.

Modern archaeological scholarship has pretty much universally rejected the historical veracity of the Exodus story and subsequent related events on the basis that there is no evidence that the Hebrew people lived in Egypt during this period. However, more recent scholarship suggests that there is significant evidence to the contrary.

The majority of this evidence centers around the excavation of the ancient settlement of Avaris in northern Egypt. The dig has revealed that this was one of the largest cities in the ancient world with an estimated population of between twenty-five thousand and thirty thousand people.[2]

Remains have been found at several sites, including tombs, pottery, and weapons. The architecture and character of the finds point to these people being non-Egyptian, Semitic people who originated from Canaan and Syria.[3]

Some of the more remarkable discoveries of the dig originated from one particular site. These include the following:

1. A north Syrian house
2. An Egyptian palace designed for a high official of state with a portico with twelve pillars
3. Twelve tombs surrounding the palace with one pyramid tomb designated for a high official of state
4. The remnants of a large statue within the pyramid tomb resembling an Asiatic person (someone of non-Egyptian origin) with a multicolored coat[4]
5. An empty pyramid tomb with an alternative tunneled entrance with no trace of bones[5]

What does all this mean? All these buildings and fixtures on one site would seem to match very well with the biblical record of the Hebrew people settling in Egypt. First, the north Syrian house is the type of house that someone like Jacob (Abraham's grandson, Joseph's father) might construct given that he spent twenty years of his life in Haran (region of north Syria). Second, the building of an Egyptian palace for a high state official with twelve pillars would seem to be an ideal residence for Joseph who was a high-state official in Egypt and was one of Jacob's twelve sons, which is possibly reflected by the existence of the twelve pillars within the palace.

Third, the pyramid tomb would be a fitting resting place for a high-state official like Joseph. Add to that the existence of a statue that resembles the biblical description of Joseph, the absence of bones indicating that the remains may have been removed, and it's all starting to look like a strong resemblance to the biblical record.

Given the potential significance here, why have these findings not garnered more attention from biblical advocates? The internet is filled with Christian

CHAPTER 3: SHOULD WE TAKE THE BIBLE SERIOUSLY?

whack jobs jumping to massively premature conclusions on the barest of evidence. I would have thought they would be all over this one. In this instance, there is a very strong vein of Egyptologists that believe that the Semitic people in Avaris appear there centuries too early to be connected to the events of the Exodus. Therefore, they deduce that it's unlikely that these are the same people who are recorded in the Bible.[6]

If you do any sort of investigation into archaeology, you will quickly discover that the establishment of timelines is a notoriously contested and constantly evolving area. It is really hard to pin down the exact timing of events. While we cannot say that the findings from Avaris are certainly the remains of the early Israelites, we can now say that there is evidence of Semitic people living in ancient Egypt. Therefore, I think it prudent that we leave ourselves open to the idea that the biblical record of Jacob, Joseph, and subsequent events shouldn't be quickly dismissed as mere fiction.

Figure 1. Behind the palace at Avaris -
12 special graves and memorial chapels built above them
Credit: Patterns of Evidence: The Exodus. Used with permission.

Figure 2. Statue of Asiatic Man – Cairo Museum (The Basement)
Credit: David Rohl. Used with permission.

Jericho

The Israelites were in the desert for approximately forty years after the supposed Exodus from slavery in Egypt. Joshua, a protégé of Moses, received the following instruction from God:

> March around the city once with all the armed men. Do this for six days. Have seven priests carry trumpets of rams' horns in front of the ark. On the seventh day, march around the city seven times, with the priests blowing the trumpets. When you hear them sound a long blast on the trumpets, have the whole army give a loud shout; then the wall of the city will collapse and the army will go up, everyone straight in. (Joshua 6:3–5)

The story goes that Joshua is obedient to the Lord: "When the trumpets sounded, the army shouted, and at the sound of the trumpet, when the men gave a loud shout, the wall collapsed; so everyone charged straight in, and they took the city" (Joshua 6:20).

CHAPTER 3: SHOULD WE TAKE THE BIBLE SERIOUSLY?

Hmm, all very believable right? Well, let's see what the archaeological evidence tells us about Jericho.

Archaeologists have excavated what they believe to be the city of Old Testament Jericho, which is located in modern-day Israel. The site has been excavated several times over the past century; British archaeologist Kathleen Kenyon performed the most notable excavation.[7] These excavations have found evidence of a fallen city wall and an intense fire,[8] which appear to support the biblical account. There is conjecture among scholars regarding the date of this supposed invasion and destruction, and whether this matches the biblical chronology. However, as previously discussed, chronologies can be very difficult to establish and one needs to keep an open mind to the consistently evolving archaeological landscape.

Figure 3. Aerial view of Jericho, Tell es-Sultan, from the west
Credit: William Schlegel/BiblePlaces.com. Used with permission.

Conquest of Lachish

If you walk into room 10B of the British Museum today, you will see a vast array of Assyrian reliefs (stone panels) that were found in the nineteenth century in northern Iraq.[9] These reliefs vividly depict the siege of the Judean city of Lachish in 701 BC by the Assyrian king, Sennacherib,[10] an event that is referred to in Old Testament writings.[11] These reliefs once adorned the walls of a small room behind the throne in the Assyrian palace in Nineveh. The British Museum has redisplayed the reliefs to mimic the order of their original placement in the palace.[12]

Black Obelisk of Shalmaneser III

Austen Henry Layard discovered the Black Obelisk of Shalmaneser III in 1846 in his excavations of the royal residence of Shalmaneser III at Nimrud, Iraq. The two-meter tall obelisk is shaped like a ziggurat, containing twenty panels on a four-sided frieze chiseled into its alabaster surface, and it has been dated to 828–827 BC. The inscription records King Shalmaneser III's military campaigns; each panel contains a scene showing the five conquered territories paying tribute to the Assyrian king with an inscription identifying those in the scene and its purpose. In one panel, the inscription mentions and depicts the Israelite King Jehu giving homage and presenting gifts to Shalmaneser, who is seated and holding a tribute vessel.

The event depicted by the Black Obelisk somewhat corroborates the biblical record of Israel's history of the ninth century BC, when the Neo-Assyrian Empire began applying pressure against Israel and Syria. The Assyrians sought territorial expansion through war, so Israel joined a coalition with Damascus and local confederacies to oppose Assyria. The coalition failed, but Jehu (previously a military leader) overthrew the Omride Dynasty and usurped the throne.[13] In 841 BC, Shalmaneser invaded Syria and forced Hazael of Damascus to pay tribute. Rather than fight Assyria, King Jehu surrendered and gained its protection. The payment made by Jehu to the Assyrian monarch depicted on the Black Obelisk is not recorded in the biblical account of his exploits.[14] The obelisk is currently held in the British Museum.[15]

CHAPTER 3: SHOULD WE TAKE THE BIBLE SERIOUSLY?

Figure 4. Lachish reliefs room - British Museum
Credit: Todd Bolen/BiblePlaces.com. Used with permission.

Figure 5. Black Obelisk of Shalmaneser III,
Side C, 858-824 BC - British Museum
Credit: Todd Bolen/BiblePlaces.com. Used with permission.

Figure 6. Black Obelisk, Side A,
Jehu of Israel bowing down - British Museum
Credit: Todd Bolen/BiblePlaces.com. Used with permission.

Exile

One of the key pinnacle events of the Old Testament is the exile of the Jewish people to the land of Babylon, which started in 597 BC and culminated in the destruction of the temple in Jerusalem in 586 BC.[16] In this period the famous Bible stories of Daniel in the lions' den and Shadrach, Meshach, and Abednego are said to have taken place.[17]

Figure 7. Babylonian Chronicle, 605-594 BC, Jerusalem capture – British Museum
Credit: Todd Bolen/BiblePlaces.com. Used with permission.

Babylonian Chronicle of the Early Years of Nebuchadnezzar

In the British Museum you can see the tablet of the Babylonian Chronicle of the Early Years of Nebuchadnezzar, which chronicles Babylonian history from 605 BC to 594 BC. The tablet describes the Babylonian King Nebuchadnezzar's first campaign against Jerusalem in 597 BC while also covering the period of twelve years from the twenty-first year of Nabopolassar (605 BC, which was also Nebuchadnezzar's accession year), through to the eleventh year of Nebuchadnezzar's reign.[18]

The tablet states the following:

> In the seventh year [598/597 BC], the month Kislev, the king of Akkad [i.e., Nebuchadnezzar] mustered his troops, marched to the Hatti-land, and encamped against the city of Judah and on the second day of the month of Adar he seized the city and captured the king. He appointed there a king of his own choice, received its heavy tribute and sent [them] to Babylon.[19]

In summation, the scribes of Nebuchadnezzar stated that Jerusalem was conquered and the defeated peoples of Judah were taken to Babylon in 597 BC, which corroborates the biblical account.[20]

King Jehoiachin Ration Tablet

Another archaeological piece that testifies to the existence of Israelites in Babylonian exile is currently being held in the Pergamon Museum in Berlin. Several clay tablets were found by Robert Koldewey in a royal archive room of King Nebuchadnezzar near the Ishtar Gate during his excavation of Babylon from 1899 to 1917. These tablets, dating from 595 to 570 BC, now known as the Babylonian Chronicles, outline the rations that were given to the Babylonian prisoners. Four of these tablets list rations of oil and barley given to various individuals, including the deposed Judean King Jehoiachin. They outline that King Nebuchadnezzar gave these rations from the royal storehouses five years after Jehoiachin was taken captive. In 2 Kings 25:27-30 it says that Jehoiachin was a prisoner of Babylon, later released and given provisions by the king of Babylon. The clay ration tablets seeming to confirm the accuracy of the biblical account.[21]

Figure 8. Jehoiachin Ration Tablet - Pergamon Museum
Credit: Ferrell Jenkins/BiblePlaces.com. Used with permission.

In addition to this, there is a substantial amount of other Mesopotamian texts that testify to the presence of Jewish people, both high-born and low-born, who lived productively in the region of Babylon right from the start of the Judean exile to the rebuilding of the temple and beyond.[22]

Post Exile: Cyrus Cylinder

The Bible recounts that Cyrus the Great, who conquered Babylon in 539 BC,[23] allowed the Jews to return to their homeland uninhibited following their period of Babylonian captivity.[24] In 1879, Hormuzd Rassam discovered the Cyrus Cylinder in the remains of the Babylonian temple of Marduk. The barrel-shaped cylinder stone is inscribed in cuneiform and details the capture of Babylon by Cyrus and his release of the captured people remaining there.

The cylinder inscription communicates that Cyrus was a worshipper of Marduk who strove for peace in Babylon and abolished the labor-service of its population. It further claims that Babylon restored the temples and religious cults of those people from neighboring countries who brought tribute to Babylon and returned their previously deported gods and people.[25] This inscription seems to corroborate with the biblical account that the Israelites were liberated from Babylon and allowed to return to their homeland.

Figure 9. Cyrus Cylinder – British Museum
*Credit: Todd Bolen/BiblePlaces.com.
Used with permission.*

A Reliable Chronology

In the Old Testament books of 1 Kings, 2 Kings, and 1 Chronicles, we find the following listing:

1. Nineteen kings of Israel
2. Twenty kings and a queen in Judah
3. Twenty-one foreign ruling contemporaries

For an illustration of these rulers in chronological order, please see Appendix 1.

Of all the foreign rulers referred to in this part of the Bible, all but two have duly turned up in other external records that have been found to date. Of the Israelite kings, nine have been evidenced in other external sources. This might sound like a low proportion, but given the Egyptian custom of not acknowledging foreign rulers who they considered hostile, this doesn't seem as inadequate. Of the Judaean kings, eight have been mentioned in external sources and several others have been referenced in archaeological discoveries.

In summation, the timeline order of the foreign kings here is impeccably accurate, as is the order of the Hebrew rulers, as evidenced by external sources. The elaborate datelines show a very high degree of consistency and reliability. All in all, the basic presentation of almost 350 years of the history of the Hebrew twin kingdoms dovetails very well with other external sources that we currently have.[26]

New Testament

Let us now turn to the New Testament. What does the archaeological record suggest about the text's supposed historicity?

The Ossuary of Caiaphas

In 1990, a tomb cave was accidentally discovered while workmen were making a water park in the Peace Forest in the southern part of Jerusalem on a hill traditionally known as the Mount of Evil Counsel (inspired by Caiaphas's words in John 11:48–50 that led to Jesus's death). Inside they found twelve ossuaries, which are boxes used to store bones. Among these twelve was one particularly ornate ossuary decorated with traces of bright orange paint and elaborate etchings of rosettes and acanthus leaves (typical of wealthier Jewish burials). Inside were the bones of two infants, two teenage boys, an adult woman, and a man of approximately sixty years of age. The text "Joseph bar Cipha" was etched on the long side, and "Joseph bar Caipha" was etched on the narrow side of the ossuary. Archaeologists generally agree that this inscription refers to the high priest Caiaphas,[27] who was a notable figure in the trial of Jesus preceding his eventual execution.[28]

Figure 10. Ossuary of Joseph son of Caiaphas, from Jerusalem, 1st century AD – Israel Museum
Credit: Todd Bolen/BiblePlaces.com. Used with permission.

Pilate Stone

Pontius Pilate was the Roman governor who presided over Jesus's crucifixion.[29] In 1961, the Italian archaeologist Antonio Frova discovered an inscription at Caesarea Maritima on a two-foot by three-foot limestone slab that was being used as a section of steps leading into the Caesarea theatre. The inscription, written over three lines, dates from AD 26 to 37, placing it during Pilate's rule. The slab is partially broken, and it reads in Latin:

[ ]S TIBERIEUM *(Tiberieum)*
[PO]NTIUS PILATUS *(Pontius Pilate)*
[PRAEF]ECTUS IUDA[EA]E *(Prefect of Judea)*

Albeit damaged, the first line probably mentions a temple to the divine Augustus, dedicated in honor of the Emperor Tiberius. The second line refers to Pilate and the third identifies him as the prefect of Judea. The slab is the only provenanced archaeological evidence of the existence of Pilate, and although his historical existence has never seriously been challenged, the discovery of this inscription solidifies his standing as a historical figure.[30]

figure 11. Pontius Pilate limestone dedicatory inscription, 26-36 AD, from Caesarea - Israel Museum

Credit: Todd Bolen/BiblePlaces.com. Used with permission.

Pool of Siloam

In the biblical book of John, a story is told about Jesus healing a blind man at the Pool of Siloam.[31] In 2004, construction work was being carried out to repair a large water pipe south of Jerusalem's Temple Mount. At the southern end of the ridge known as the City of David, the archaeologists Ronny Reich and Eli Shukron identified two ancient stone steps. Further excavation revealed a significant pool structure from the second temple period, which is the period when Jesus supposedly lived. The pool is very large at approximately seventy meters long and is trapezoidal in shape.[32] While we cannot be conclusively sure that this is the actual Pool of Siloam referred to in the book of John, no one seems to be opposing the theory either. Therefore, it seems reasonable to conclude that this discovery could very well be the Pool of Siloam referenced in the Bible.

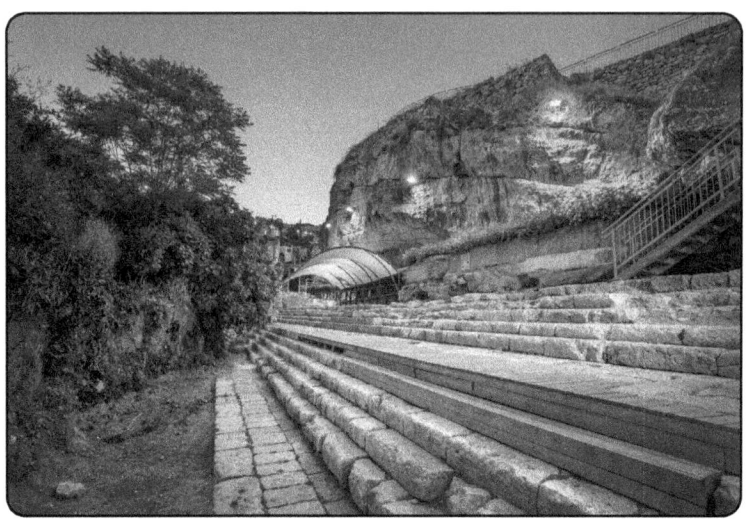

Figure 12. Northern perimeter of the Pool of Siloam – Jerusalem. At the date of publication the full site is in the process of being fully excavated.
Credit: Koby Harati, City of David Archives. Used with permission.

Figure 13. Rendering of the Pool of Siloam, second temple period
Credit: Shalom Kveller, City of David Archives. Used with permission.

Records of Biblical Characters

To date, fifty-three people from the biblical record have been identified in archaeological finds.[33] When compared to the total number of people recorded in the Bible (estimated to be some three thousand people),[34] it's a very small percentage. However, I think to view the Bible in a lesser historical light based on this is to misunderstand the constraints of archaeology.

Archaeology can only comment on what it finds, not what it doesn't find. The absence of archaeological evidence cannot equate to evidence of absence. As each day passes, more and more excavations are revealing more and more about the biblical period, and we're probably only just scratching the surface. For instance, of the thousands of known surviving ancient sites, only a fraction have been surveyed, much less excavated. Less than 1 percent of ancient Egypt has been discovered and excavated, despite the preeminent attention paid to this site since the beginning of archaeology as a discipline.[35]

In Summary

The archaeological examples that I have just discussed are a sample of a much larger pool of discoveries that have been made to date. One can take a closer look at all of these individual discoveries, and there are many of them. However, one cannot conclusively say that any of these discoveries confirm the Bible or prove that it communicates actual history. To place any sort of expectation of this nature on the discipline of archaeology is to fundamentally misunderstand its limitations.

What I hope to have demonstrated here is that the evidence discovered to date regarding the Bible should stop us from too easily dismissing its historicity and significance. To initially dismiss it as a work of fiction like *Harry Potter* isn't a fair treatment of the text given what evidence we have in our hands. If the Bible were true, then I think that the archaeological evidence that we have sourced to date would be the sort of evidence that we would reasonably expect to find given the current technologies available. Would we like more evidence? Of course, and the digging continues.

ii. Manuscript Transmission
We Can Be Confident That the Bible in Our Possession Today Is Very Close in Wording to the Original Manuscripts

We have so far examined the case for the Bible's validity to communicate history, but we must now turn our attention to the very practical matter of textual criticism. Textual criticism is the discipline that attempts to determine the original wording of any document when the original is no longer in existence.[36]

The Bible as we have it today is a collection of books that have been copied for thousands of years. How do we know whether these books have been copied accurately through the ages? Surely given the elapsed time, there would have been errors and modifications made during transfer that make the book and its claims substantially unreliable.

In order to examine this question properly we need to have a reasonable understanding of what the literary landscape looked like during biblical times. We type an electronic message at a moment's notice, but this couldn't be further from what ancient writers experienced.

For an example, let's take the Dead Sea Scrolls, which are arguably the greatest archaeological find of the twentieth century.[37] The primary material of the biblical scrolls is parchment.[38] Parchment is a greatly refined form of leather from the skins of various animals such as cattle, sheep, and goats. The production process involves washing the skin and removing the hair or wool. The skin is stretched tight on a frame, scraped thin to remove further traces of hair and flesh, whitened with chalk, and smoothed with pumice.[39]

As you can see from this small snapshot, the process of farming, procuring, and writing on parchment was no doubt more time-consuming and expensive than the modern writing methods we utilize today. It is reasonable to deduce that a writer would be far more selective in what they wrote or copied given the significant investment required to do so. In respect to copying, it would also be reasonable to presume that the copier would be more diligent to ensure accuracy given the significant time required to correct errors.

So, does this presumption stand up to the available evidence?

Old Testament

Before the discovery of the Dead Sea Scrolls in 1947, English translations of the Old Testament were based almost exclusively on the Masoretic Text (MT). The MT was a text produced by a Jewish scribal group called the Masoretes who meticulously copied the Hebrew Bible, predominantly during the sixth through the eleventh centuries AD. More than three thousand manuscripts transcribed from the 1100s to 1440 currently survive. The oldest complete copy of the MT is the Leningrad Codex, which has been dated to AD 1008.[40]

If you know your Old Testament timeline, you won't take much comfort from the MT as these copies were made more than one thousand years after the Old Testament documents were written. That seems like a really long gap. However, the discovery of the Dead Sea Scrolls was a game changer in this regard.[41]

In 1947, Bedouin shepherds discovered seven scrolls near a site called Khirbet Qumran. These scrolls were sold, and eventually they found their way into the hands of scholars. This led to many subsequent excavations in the area and yielded the discovery of approximately 930 manuscripts, which are commonly referred to today as the Dead Sea Scrolls. Most of the scrolls were made of leather, a few of papyrus, and one of copper.[42]

Of the total manuscripts found, 23 percent were books of the Old Testament (213 manuscripts).[43] These have been dated from 250 BC to AD 50.[44] All the books of the Old Testament are represented in the find (except for Esther and Nehemiah),[45] and what makes these texts so significant is how similar they are to the Masoretic texts of a millennium or more later. The clearest example of this was the discovery of an entire scroll of Isaiah that contained only a handful of extremely minor differences in content to the MT copies.[46]

In summary, the discovery of the Dead Sea Scrolls demonstrated that the transmission of the Old Testament was done to a very high standard.

Another reason that some put forward to authenticate the Old Testament writings is that Jesus himself validated the literature. If you accept that Jesus was God, and he accepted the Old Testament writings as valid, then you would accordingly have to accept them as well.[47] Obviously this argument hinges on one accepting that Jesus is God and this will be considered in upcoming chapters.

New Testament

There is a significant number of New Testament manuscripts we can analyze to see whether the documents were transmitted accurately through the ages. Compared to other documents of antiquity, the New Testament is well out in front in terms of sheer quantity of manuscripts.

In addition to the Greek manuscripts of the New Testament, there are another 18,130 manuscripts of early translations that we can draw upon to ascertain the text's integrity.

In terms of variation, some scholars estimate at the higher end of the spectrum that there are some four hundred thousand textual variants spread across the twenty-five thousand manuscripts in existence today. It sounds like a considerable number. That works out to an average of sixteen variants per manuscript.[48]

At this point we need to define what we mean by "variant." Scholars differentiate between accidental variants and intentional ones. Accidental variants would include:

- Misspellings
- Duplicating or omitting a letter, word, or line of text
- Dividing words that were originally run together without spacing
- Placing punctuation in different places

Table 1: Manuscript Data from the Ancient World

Work	Estimated Date of Authorship	Estimated Date of Earliest Copy	Estimated Number of Copies
New Testament Greek Manuscripts	AD 55 to 100	AD 130 (or earlier)	5,300[49]
Homer's Iliad	730 BC[50]	415 BC	1,900+
Livy's History of Rome	29 BC[51] to AD 17[52]	4th century AD	About 473
Demosthenes's Speeches	340 to 330 BC[53]	1st century BC, possibly earlier	444
Caesar's Gallic Wars	58 to 52 BC[54]	9th century AD	251
Plato's Tetralogies	427 to 347 BC[55]	3rd century BC	238
Sophocles's Plays	468 to 406 BC[56]	3rd century BC	About 226
Pliny the Elder's Natural History	AD 77[57]	5th century AD	200+
Thucydides's History	431 to 395 BC[58]	3rd century BC	188
Herodotus's History	440 to 420 BC[59]	150 to 50 BC	About 106
Tacitus's Annals	AD 100 to 111[60]	First half: AD 850 Second half: AD 1050	36

Table adapted from McDowell, Evidence that Demands a Verdict, 52, 56.

Scribes were obviously human, and they were prone to mistakes just like typists were in the twentieth century.

Intentional variants are more interesting to analyze as they appear to show a scribe making an intentional change to the text. Such changes could be made for a variety of reasons:

- Perhaps a scribe was copying a well known passage but the wording was not as he or she remembered it and thus made a change.
- In the scribe's mind, there was a glaring error such as a grammatical, geographical, or historical faux pas, and they felt compelled to correct it.
- The scribe didn't like the essence of the passage and decided to alter its overall meaning.[61]

This all sounds rather disconcerting, doesn't it? The sheer number of errors and the supposed intentional nature of some doesn't leave us with a great sense of confidence that we could ever have a truly accurate Bible.

Given that there is a large number of New Testament manuscripts, very detailed analysis and scholarship can and has been performed to determine whether these variations materially affect the true essence of the Bible. In summary, this scholarship tells us the following:

- It is estimated that the vast majority of these variations focus upon 6 percent of the New Testament text.
- Less than 3 percent of variations are significant enough to be presented in one of the two standard critical editions of the Greek New Testament.
- About a tenth of 1 percent are interesting enough to make their way into footnotes in most English translations.

In summary, New Testament scholars consistently arrive at the conclusion that no orthodox doctrine or ethical practice of Christianity depends solely on any disputed wording. The New Testament scholar and skeptic Bart Ehrman, who authored *Misquoting Jesus: The Story Behind Who Changed the Bible and Why*, admits in this very book that "essential Christian beliefs are not affected by textual variants in the manuscript tradition of the New Testament."[62]

A period of silence, however...

On October 1, 2011, two heavyweight scholars of New Testament textual criticism took to the floor to debate whether we can trust the text of the New Testament. Bart Ehrman argued for the negative and Daniel Wallace for the affirmative.

Ehrman's chief challenge to Wallace in the debate was that we have virtually no New Testament manuscripts from the time of original authorship (circa AD 50 to 100) until the end of the second century. Therefore, we have no way of knowing if and how much corruption of the texts took place during this early period (see figure below).[63]

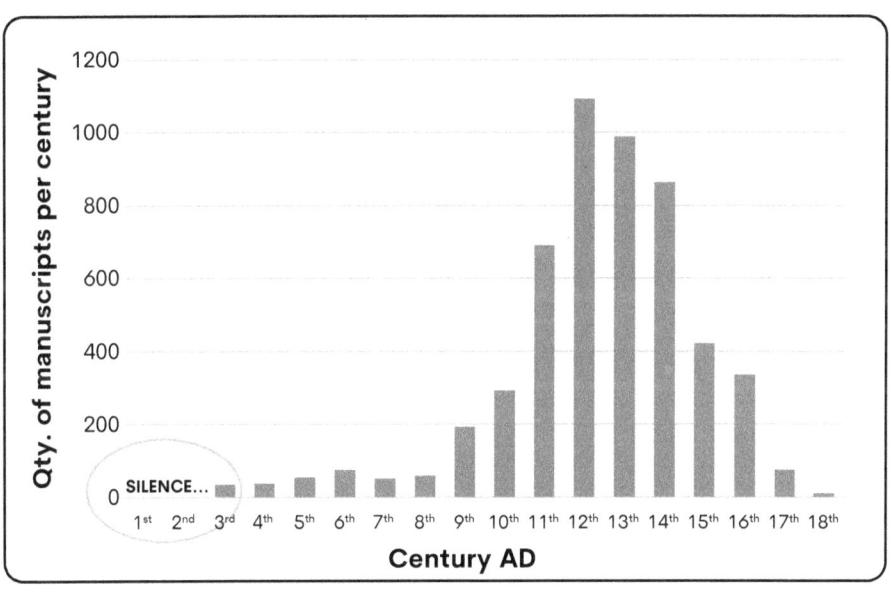

Figure 14. Distribution of New Testament manuscripts by century
Source: Aland, The Text of the New Testament, 82.

Ehrman is right. In theory, there could have been loads of corruption during this earlier period, which was then followed by a period of stable textual transmission. How then can anyone be confident that the extant New Testament accurately records the events of the supposed time?

The short answer is that you cannot be 100 percent confident that the New Testament was reliably transmitted through this period. At the same time, you cannot be equivalently confident that it wasn't transmitted accurately through this period. How does one navigate this road with seemingly two divergent cliff faces on either side?

The greater wealth of manuscript data conveys that the Bible has been reliably transmitted through a substantial period, some two thousand years in total. We know from our earlier analysis that the Old Testament writings have been reliably transmitted to today from copies made as early as 250 BC. Are we then going to instinctively hypothesize that copyists copied the Old Testament correctly from 250 BC through to the end of second century, but for some unknown reason the copyists (the same or different) didn't copy the New Testament to the same degree of accuracy? It would seem to me that the prudent and most reasonable assumption to make in this instance is that in all likelihood the copyists copied the New Testament documents with a similar degree of accuracy. To assert that the New Testament texts were corrupted in this two-hundred-year period is to make a leap of faith with little evidence.

Would we like more evidence from this period in question? Sure, we would. But the absence of accurate New Testament transmission evidence through this period cannot equate to the evidence of absence. In dealing with the ancient world, we must be prepared to make allowances that we just don't have to make in today's modern landscape.

It is also worth noting that the New Testament's gap from the date of authorship to the earliest manuscript is one of the narrowest in the world of ancient texts. Please see Table 2, adjacent.

Table 2: Time Gap from Estimated Date of Authorship to Earliest Manuscript

Work	Time Gap from Estimated Date of Authorship to Earliest Manuscript (Years)
Caesar's Gallic Wars	852
Tacitus's Annals	750
Pliny the Elder's Natural History	323
Homer's Iliad	315
Livy's History of Rome	283
Herodotus's History	270
Demosthenes's Speeches	230
Sophocles's Plays	106
Thucydides's History	95
New Testament Greek Manuscript	75
Plato's Tetralogies	47

Table adapted from McDowell, Evidence that Demands a Verdict, 56, with additional data incorporated.

iii. Historical Credibility
The Accounts of Jesus's Life and Resurrection Were Written Sufficiently Close Enough to the Events to Lend Them Historical Credibility

A common charge against the claimed resurrection of Jesus and the broader bibliography of his life is that the biblical accounts were published far too long after the events. It is estimated that the biblical accounts were published between thirty-eight to one hundred years after the events they report on. In our modern age, this sounds like an eternity.

In order to evaluate this properly, one must consider how we ascertain any sort of history in the ancient world. Table 3 (pp. 36–37) outlines a list of significant ancient documents that are regarded as historical in nature and shows how long after the claimed events they were published.

As you can see, some documents are written closer to the historical events than the New Testament documents, while others are written much later (such as Livy's History of Rome and the Iliad). This can be more effectively demonstrated in Figure 15 (following page).

It is interesting to compare the biblical accounts and the writings of Suetonius, both of which are biographical in nature. Suetonius's work has been described as largely responsible for providing a vivid picture of Roman society and its leaders that has dominated historical thought, albeit modified in modern times by the discovery of non-literary evidence.[64]

Tamsyn Barton, in her introduction to the *Lives of the Twelve Caesars,* says of Suetonius:

> "In the absence of other literary historical sources which are at all close to contemporary—apart from the great Tacitus—Suetonius' work is a key source of information about the Roman Empire.... He [Suetonius] is seen to have provided fascinating insights into the society and culture of his day. By comparison with the highly colored Tacitus, he seems to many an 'objective' source."[65]

CHAPTER 3: SHOULD WE TAKE THE BIBLE SERIOUSLY?

Given that Suetonius's writings are valued for their picture of history, should we dismiss the gospel writings as unreliable solely because they were written too far from the supposed historical events? Suetonius wrote about Caesar and Augustus much later after their reigns than the biblical writers wrote about Jesus.

In respect to the other ancient sources, Herodotus has been called the "father of history,"[66] and he is considered the leading source of historical information for Greece and much of western Asia and Egypt.[67] He published 54 to 125 years after the events took place—a gap wider than that of the gospel accounts. Tacitus is widely regarded as one of the most famous Roman historians,[68] and he wrote his Annals with a similar historical gap to the gospels. Livy is regarded as Rome's greatest historian,[69] and at a bare minimum he wrote history 144 years after the event, up to 676 years in some cases.

All in all, I think to dismiss the biblical accounts of Jesus on the basis of their delayed recording is to fundamentally dismiss the method and discipline of ancient history. That is fine if you wish to do so. However, if you are comfortable with the idea that we can know and ascertain the history of the Roman and Hellenistic Empires, then you arguably should be more than comfortable that the history of Jesus of Nazareth can be attested to as well.

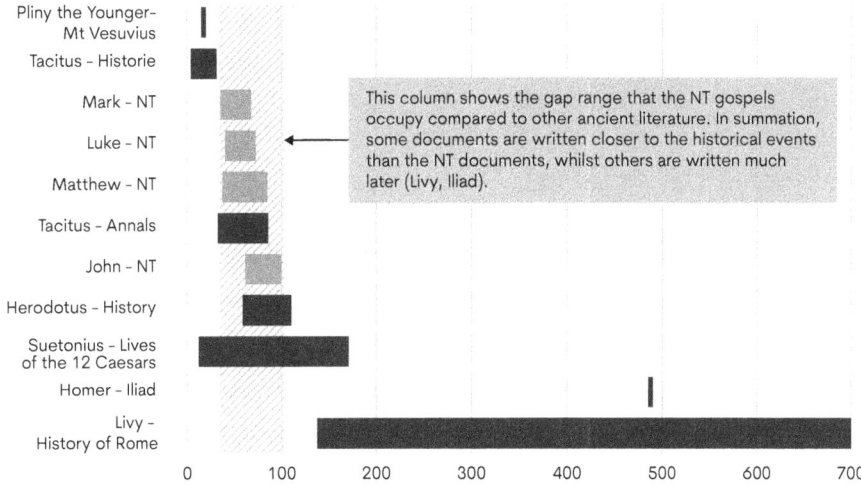

Figure 15. Time distance of publication from the historical event

Table 3: Time Gap from the Historical Event to the Earliest Manuscript Published

Work	Estimated Date of Publication	Areas Covered	Estimated Gap Between the Claimed Historical Events and the Earliest Estimated Date of Publication (Years)
Book of Matthew – New Testament	AD 70 to 85[70]	Biographical account of the life of Jesus (AD 0 to 33)	37–85
Book of Mark – New Testament	AD 68[71]	Biographical account of the life of Jesus (AD 0 to 33)	35–68
Book of Luke – New Testament	Late 60s AD to late 70s AD[72]	Biographical account of the life of Jesus (AD 0 to 33)	40–73
Book of John – New Testament	AD 90 to 100[73]	Biographical account of the life of Jesus (AD 0 to 33)	62–100
Homer – Iliad	730 BC[74]	The legendary conflict of the Trojan War (estimated period of occurrence is 1220 BC)[75]	490
Livy – History of Rome	29 BC[76] to AD 17[77]	The foundation of Rome (began in 753 BC[78] up until the battle of Pydna in 167 BC)[79]	138–724

Caesar – Gallic Wars	58 to 52 BC[80]	Gallic Wars (58 to 49 BC)[81]	Minimal
Thucydides – History of the Peloponnesian War	431 to 397 BC[82]	The Peloponnesian War (431 to 404 BC)[83]	Minimal
Herodotus – History	440 to 420 BC[84]	Ionian revolt (499 to 494 BC)[85] Battle of Marathon (490 BC)[86] Growth and organization of the Persian Empire and a description of its geography, social structure, and history (up until 550 BC)[87]	59–110
Tacitus – Annals	AD 100 to 111[88]	Roman Empire (AD 14 to 68)[89]	32–86
Tacitus – Histories	AD 100 to 111[90]	Roman Empire (AD 69 to 96)[91]	4–31
Pliny the Younger – Mount Vesuvius	AD 99 to 109[92]	Pliny gave an account of the Vesuvius eruption (AD 79[93]) to Tacitus for his Histories[94]	20
Suetonius – Lives of the Twelve Caesars	AD 120[95]	Biographical accounts of twelve Roman emperors (starting with Caesar in 49 BC to Domitian in AD 96)[96]	24–171

iv. Undiluted Motives

There Is No Serious Evidence to Suggest That Any of the Biblical Writings Were Engineered by Authority Figures to Exercise Control

A very common accusation I hear is that the Bible was engineered by authority figures to exert control over the masses. I've never encountered serious, substantial evidence to support this claim. However, it's perfectly responsible and necessary to explore how the books of the Bible came to be selected and recognized as authoritative while others were not.

Part of me loves the idea that when people had finally come to grips with Jesus's death and supposed resurrection a group of key religious leaders all sat down at a roundtable and unanimously decided which books were to be included as "Holy Scripture" once and for all. It would certainly make the origins of the Bible a lot easier to explain. However, the actual history of how these books came together is far more complicated.

First, let's consider the formulation of the Old Testament.

Old Testament

In short, we cannot point to a specific moment in time when the collection of books known as the Old Testament was first established. I appreciate that this makes for uncomfortable reading. However, one does learn that eliciting history from the ancient world is more of a process of deciding what is more likely to have happened, rather than establishing definitively what has happened.

With that said, I will now outline what can be reasonably deduced regarding the establishment of the Old Testament.

When Jesus began his public ministry, he often referred to and fielded questions from religious leaders about "the Law and the Prophets." We cannot

CHAPTER 3: SHOULD WE TAKE THE BIBLE SERIOUSLY?

say definitively what "the Law and the Prophets" represents in exact detail. The Jewish historian Josephus wrote toward the end of the first century AD in his *Against Apion*:[97]

> Naturally, then, or rather necessarily – seeing that it is not open to anyone to write of their own accord, nor is there any disagreement present in what is written, but the prophets alone learned, by inspiration from God, what had happened in the distant and most ancient past and recorded plainly events in their own time just as they occurred – among us there are not thousands of books in disagreement and conflict with each other, but only twenty-two books, containing the record of all time, which are rightly trusted. Five of these are the books of Moses, which contain both the laws and the tradition from the birth of humanity up to his death; this is a period of a little less than 3,000 years. From the death of Moses until Artaxerxes, king of the Persians after Xerxes, the prophets after Moses wrote the history of what took place in their own times in thirteen books; the remaining four books contain hymns to God and instructions for people on life. From Artaxerxes up to our own time every event has been recorded, but this is not judged worthy of the same trust, since the exact line of succession of the prophets did not continue. It is clear in practice how we approach our own writings. Although such a long time has now passed, no-one has dared to add, to take away, or to alter anything; and it is innate in every Judean, right from birth, to regard them as decrees of God, to remain faithful to them and, if necessary, gladly to die on their behalf.[98]

To summarize, Josephus claimed the following:

1. Twenty-two books were deemed authoritative in the religious life of the Jewish people.
2. This collection of books was finalized around the middle of the fourth century BC, during the reign of the Persian King Artaxerxes (465 to 424 BC).[99]
3. Other books were written from the reign of King Artaxerxes to the writing of this work from Josephus (circa AD 100), but none of those other books were added to this Jewish collection.

Of the twenty-two books that Josephus referenced, some argue that he was almost certainly referring to the Old Testament books that we read in our modern day Protestant Bible.[100] He referred to the five books of Moses:

1. Genesis
2. Exodus
3. Leviticus
4. Numbers
5. Deuteronomy

He then referred to thirteen books written by the prophets:

6. Job
7. Joshua
8. Judges
9. Samuel
10. Kings
11. Isaiah
12. Jeremiah
13. Ezekiel
14. The Twelve
15. Daniel
16. Chronicles
17. Ezra-Nehemiah
18. Esther

And the remaining four books were probably the following:

19. Psalms
20. Proverbs
21. Song of Songs
22. Ecclesiastes

That's the twenty-two. One cannot be 100 percent confident that Josephus was referring to these books; however, an examination of the broader context of the period seems to indicate that, in all likelihood, he was. Josephus referred to three categories of Scripture:

1. The books of Moses
2. The books of the prophets
3. The remaining books of hymns

Other ancient works of this period refer to other writings as "sacred" or "scripture," and they are labeled in a similar tripartite form.[101] Again, while we cannot conclude that all these references refer to the same writings, the similar labeling should help us be open to the possibility that a consistent, well known collection was at play here. To date, there have been no other writings found that materially contest Josephus's delineation of the Jewish Scripture of the period that he refers to. All of these pieces lead me to think that there was an established corpus of Jewish writings during the ancient period and that in all likelihood these correspond to the traditional Hebrew Scriptures.

However, if you remember my opening preamble at the start of the chapter, I said that there were thirty-nine books in our modern day Old Testament. Why the discrepancy here with Josephus?

From the twenty-two that Josephus referred to, there is evidence that books have been adjusted over the centuries to take the number to thirty-nine:

1. The book of Ruth was initially appended to Judges and was eventually separated out.
2. Lamentations was appended to Jeremiah and subsequently separated out.
3. The Twelve that Josephus references were probably made up of the minor prophets, which were Hosea, Joel, Amos, Obadiah, Jonah, Micah, Nahum, Habakkuk, Zephaniah, Haggai, Zechariah, and Malachi.
4. Samuel eventually split into 1 and 2 Samuel.
5. Kings eventually split into 1 and 2 Kings.
6. Chronicles eventually split into 1 and 2 Chronicles.

These delineations result in an extra seventeen books, which takes the total from twenty-two to the modern day thirty-nine.

The Catholic and Eastern Orthodox Bibles

To complicate matters further, if you open a modern day Catholic Bible or Eastern Orthodox Bible, you will see that there are forty-six and forty-nine books, respectively, in their Old Testaments. Why the discrepancies again?

Josephus referred to other recordings that took place from the time of Artaxerxes in fourth century BC to his time of writing in AD 100. However, he says that these documents were not worthy of the same trust, and as a result they were not held in the same regard as the revered collection of twenty-two by the Jewish people.

Josephus was probably referring to a series of writings known as the Apocrypha. I've outlined these in Appendix 2.

The term "Apocrypha" means "hidden" in Greek and is used to denote a collection of Jewish writings, dating from roughly 300 BC to AD 70, that are included in the Roman Catholic and Orthodox Old Testaments.[102] Eleven of the seventeen Apocryphal works are included in the Catholic Bible, while the Orthodox Old Testament incorporates all of them with 4 Maccabees and the Prayer of Manasseh listed as appendices.

In addition, Josephus could also be referring to another group of writings called the Old Testament Pseudepigrapha. These are another sixty or more books that are typically attributed to some ancient Old Testament patriarch or key figure in Jewish history who lived long before the time of the book's actual writing. With only one or two exceptions, these works were never formally recognized as authoritative, thus they were never really a point of contention in establishing a biblical collection.[103]

The Apocrypha, however, did become a contentious issue in the emerging expansion of the Christian faith. The development of the Christian Old Testament diverged from the supposed traditional Jewish collection after the two faith communities separated in the first century AD. Quotations and allusions in the New Testament writings show that the new Christian movement adopted the Jewish concept of authoritative Scripture. Passages from these books provided a theological framework for the proclamation of the Christian message and of Jesus as the promised Messiah as articulated in New Testament writings.[104]

However, most of the Christians who utilized Jewish texts used a Greek translation known as the Septuagint.[105] The early origins of the Septuagint are owed to the decree made by King Cyrus of Persia allowing Jews to resettle in their homeland following their Babylonian exile in 587 to 586 BC. Many chose to return home while many others remained in Babylon or resettled in major cities around the Mediterranean world. Jews who settled outside their traditional homeland were referred to as "Diaspora Jews" or "Jews of the Dispersion." After taking up residence in new regions, it was not long before many of the Jews forgot their native Hebrew tongue and could only communicate in the language of the lands where they had migrated.[106]

Fast forward to the era of Alexander the Great, and the Hellenization of this ancient world begins. The Hellenization program was all-encompassing and involved learning the Greek language and all other things Greek. Soon enough, many peoples throughout the Mediterranean world—including many leaders in the land of Israel—learned both the language and culture of the Greeks. Hellenization was a complex notion; several generations passed before it became the dominant socialization program of the Greco-Roman world, and its influence carried on for centuries after the demise of the Greek Empire.[107]

With Greek now the universal language of the Mediterranean world, most Diaspora Jews could no longer communicate in their native Hebrew. As such, they needed their sacred books translated into Greek.[108] Beginning around 250 BC, Jews in Egypt began to translate the Hebrew Bible into Greek to address this need. The translation process began with the first five books (Genesis, Exodus, Leviticus, Numbers, Deuteronomy) and then extended to the other books. This collection of translations was eventually called the Septuagint (related to the Latin word for "seventy")[109] owing to a legend that it had been translated individually by seventy-two people.[110]

The Septuagint was comprised of those books that became (or already were) the authorized Hebrew collection of sacred texts and the Apocrypha.[111] There is debate on whether the Jews thought of the Apocrypha as "Scripture." I think it more likely that they viewed these texts as useful references worthy of translation, in a very distinct category to the other scriptural books.

Moving forward to the period following Jesus's death, a new message was being taken throughout the Mediterranean world. Greek was the universal language, and it should come as no surprise that these new followers of Christ adopted the Septuagint as the "default Bible" of their new emerging church.[112] The writers of what would eventually become the New Testament used the Greek Septuagint almost exclusively in their work.[113] Perhaps one can now start to see the potential divergence on the horizon. On one hand, we have the Jewish faith with its sacred twenty-two books containing "the record of all time." On the other, we have this new Jesus thing spreading like wildfire throughout the Mediterranean world, with its Greek Septuagint in hand containing the Apocryphal writings. A debate on what texts should form the basis for appropriate and right theological foundation would be expected.

In the second century AD, many Jews believed that the Septuagint translation had theological problems.[114] Throw into the mix the rapidly expanding Christian movement and the destruction of the Jewish temple in AD 70, and it's not too hard to imagine that the Jewish people and faith had an identity crisis. As a result, the different factions of Judaism were replaced by the dominant Pharisee movement, which represented the future of the faith. Some argue that the Jewish collection was only then established by the second century AD (as shown by the Rabbinic literature).[115] Others (like me) argue that it is more likely the Rabbinic leadership felt it necessary to formally articulate in detail what these authorized Hebrew books were in an increasingly Septuagint-dominated landscape.

As for the new Christian movement, the process of establishing an authorized, universally recognized collection of Old Testament literature was significantly more long-winded. Western Christianity eventually became centered at Rome and developed various differences in theology and practice from their

Eastern counterparts. The alienation of the Latin Catholic West from the Greek Orthodox East eventually resulted in slight differences within their respective Old Testament collections (Appendix 3 shows that the Greek Orthodox Bible recognizes some additional books the Catholic Bible does not). While the Eastern church persisted in using the Greek Septuagint as its Old Testament, Christians in the West began to use a Latin translation known as the Vulgate. The Vulgate was translated from the original Hebrew texts by Jerome at some period from the end of the fourth century to the beginning of the fifth.[116]

Following in the footsteps of some earlier church leaders, Jerome advanced the view that books that were not found in the original Hebrew Bible should not be considered authoritative. He subsequently labeled these books "Apocrypha,"[117] which is arguably the first coining of the term for these writings.[118] Jerome's position was ultimately not adopted, but a minority of Catholic theological thinkers continued to share his view. Fast forward to the sixteenth century, and the emerging Protestant movement marginalized those books that are not found in the Hebrew Bible,[119] ultimately resulting in the Protestant Reformation's return to an Old Testament collection with only the traditional Hebrew Bible.[120] In reaction to this, the Catholic church definitively affirmed the legitimacy of seven disputed books at the Council of Trent in 1546 (see Appendix 3).[121] This is why the Catholic Bible today has more books that the Protestant Bible.

In Summary

It's fair to say that the formulation of the Old Testament was not a neat and tidy affair. The way that some Christians discuss its character, you would think that God handwrote the collection himself and there was never any question of its authenticity or completeness. Such an idea is plainly out of step with the historical record.

Alternatively, the idea that the Old Testament compilation was simply a free-for-all where multitudes of books were in and out in a never-ending rotation is not accurate either. Taking a survey of the early church fathers and the lists of books they considered authoritative shows a strong consensus around a consistent corpus, that primarily being the thirty-nine books of the Hebrew Bible (see Appendix 4).

When I step back and reflect on all of the above, I am not surprised that the Old Testament endured something of a complicated assembly. The Christian faith exploded following the supposed death and resurrection of Jesus, and this movement flung Jewish writings all over the Mediterranean to a world of differing cultures and languages. No wonder there was a significant element of trying to "figure it all out" and decide which texts were relevant and how they related to the religious and cultural disruption that Jesus brought. At the end of the day, I suspect that the Old Testament writings stayed the course because it is only with them that one can make sense of who Jesus was, what he did, and why it matters.

New Testament

After all the supposed shenanigans of the Old Testament formation, you'll be pleased to know that the New Testament takes a more straightforward path. In our modern-day Bibles, the Protestant, Orthodox, and Catholic versions all carry the exact same twenty-seven books that make up the New Testament.

So how did it take shape? Following the death, supposed resurrection, and ascension of Jesus, his followers remained based in Jerusalem. They were all Jewish, and as such, their "new church" emerged as a sect within Judaism. Stephen, one of the Hellenistic Jewish leaders of the community, was executed in AD 34[122] by the traditional Jewish authorities because he riled them up with an explosive speech that is recorded in Acts 7 of the Bible. Following this, many other Hellenistic Jews (Jews who grew up in a Hellenistic culture and spoke Greek as their first language) feared for their safety and left Jerusalem for other neighboring regions. This scattering of the Hellenistic believers from Palestine was the first instance of this "Jesus movement" moving into the non-Jewish world.[123]

The first largely Gentile (non-Jewish) church was then founded and established in the great eastern city of Antioch, which was located within the

Roman province of Syria. In Antioch, the term "Christian" was first used and the first organized Christian mission originated (AD 46[124]), which was led by the apostle Paul who became the crucial driver of Christianity into the western European world.[125]

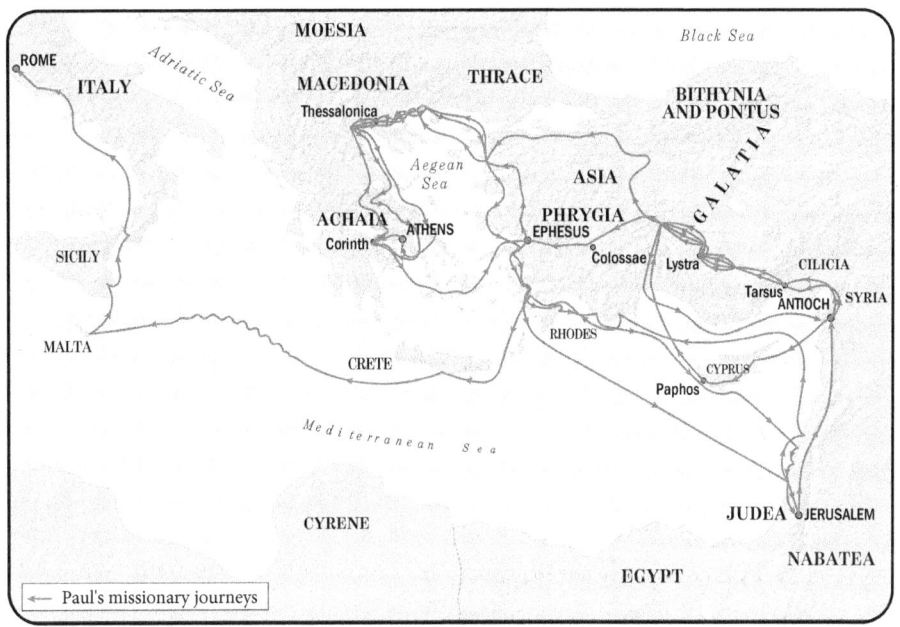

Figure 16. Paul's missionary journeys
Credit: Open.Bible/Maps. Redrawn with permission according to license @ creativecommons.org/licenses/by-sa/4.0

Paul undertook three missionary journeys within the approximate period of AD 46 to 56; these took him through Asia Minor, Greece, and Cyprus.[126] He was eventually arrested in Jerusalem in AD 57 and transported to Rome where he was executed by Emperor Nero in AD 64 or 67.[127]

The other twelve apostles' activities post-Christ are somewhat harder to piece together. The table below makes conservative estimates for where they operated in their missional endeavors, which shows them predominantly operating within the Mediterranean sphere around to Rome.

Table 4: Where the Apostles Operated

Apostle	Estimated Area of Activity
Simon Peter	He ministered in the Jerusalem church and surrounding areas. He was arrested following the execution of James by King Herod Agrippa in AD 44 and then escaped.[128] Following this, he most likely performed ministry work in Syria or Anatolia.[129] Peter also ministered in Rome and was eventually executed there by crucifixion.[130]
Andrew	The brother of Simon Peter, Andrew ministered in several regions including Scythia, Anatolia, Thrace, Macedonia, and Achaea in southern Greece, where he was eventually crucified.[131]
James (son of Zebedee)	A prominent leader in the church of Jerusalem,[132] he also possibly ministered in Antioch.[133] He was executed in AD 44 by King Herod Agrippa.[134]
John	He founded the church in Ephesus somewhere between AD 50 and 54. It is difficult to be specific regarding his later life. Eventually, he either was banished by the Romans to the island of Patmos and died there in old age, or he died in Ephesus.[135]
Philip	He potentially visited Greece, Anatolia, Palestine, Africa, and Bactria. There is a remote possibility he visited Gaul. His supposed crucifixion in Anatolia is the most commonly accepted account of his death.[136]
Bartholomew	It's difficult to establish a history for Bartholomew. Potential areas of ministry include Phrygia, India, and Armenia. Several accounts of his supposed martyrdom are put forward with no leading contenders.[137]
Thomas	He appears to have ministered in the regions of Edessa, Syria, and Armenia. There is a popular tradition that Thomas ministered and was eventually martyred in India, but this idea is probably more entrenched in legend and should be less promulgated than it typically is.[138]

Apostle	Estimated Area of Activity
Matthew	He seems to have ministered in Parthia and was eventually martyred there. He possibly also ministered in Ethiopia.[139]
James (son of Alphaeus)	It's difficult to trace his movements, but a contender is that he ministered in Parthia before dying in Ethiopia.[140]
Thaddaeus (Jude)	It seems he centered his ministry work in Armenia with some crossover into Parthia.[141]
Simon the Zealot	He likely traveled to North Africa before ministering in Persia where he was eventually martyred.[142]
Matthias	He most likely ministered in western Scythia or Parthia and possibly Ethiopia. There is no account of his death.[143]

During this immediate expansion of Christianity through the Mediterranean world by Paul and the apostles, their teachings were most likely disseminated by predominantly oral rather than written methods. While some materials are estimated to have been written down quite early (AD 50 to 65) and were probably utilized, the greater mode of transmission was likely verbal. Why was this the case?

Oral Tradition

Literacy levels in Jesus's time were very low; estimates range from 5 percent across the whole population to a possible peak of 15 percent among the urban male demographic. No printing press existed during this period, so it is virtually impossible to see how any sort of mass distribution of literature could be achieved. We can be reasonably confident that such an environment would necessitate oral transmission as the primary method of communication.[144]

Greek historians also argued that a firsthand account was preferred to the written word.[145] Given all this, is it is not surprising that the followers of this new Jesus movement knew that their primary task of spreading this "new truth" would be through physical and oral endeavors. The written word was never up to the task in this ancient context. The radical and disruptive message that a human being died and was resurrected in bodily form surely demanded the firsthand account of the person making the claim. The whites of their eyeballs would need to be seen. Their claims would need to be cross-examined scrupulously in the immediate moment.

But the Texts Come

Eventually, however, written texts started to be produced. Why might this occur?

1. **Preservation of memory:** Obviously as time progressed, the firsthand witnesses of Jesus's death and resurrection started to die off. It is natural, then, that their memories would need to be written down to preserve the teaching and messages of Christianity for future generations.
2. **Establishing core beliefs**: As the Christian community expanded around the Mediterranean world and became more diverse, the need arose to establish Christian doctrine and practice to mitigate the risk of heresies forming.
3. **Travel restrictions:** The primary writer of New Testament documents, Paul, was imprisoned several times. Naturally, then, the written method was the only way for him to communicate with the wider movement.
4. **The understanding regarding the second coming of Christ:** The original witnesses of Jesus's ministry had expected the second coming of Christ to occur in their lifetime.[146] When this didn't occur, this may have motivated the original witnesses to record their observations and other events.[147]

It seems that certain texts began to gain traction and some level of prominence within these emerging Christian communities around the Mediterranean. Appendix 5 outlines which writings the early church leaders (apostolic fathers) had in their possession and were utilizing in their worldview formulations.

What can be reasonably deduced from the data?

- By the end of the first century, Christian communities had most likely formed across the Mediterranean and in Rome.
- The Roman historians Tacitus, Suetonius, and Pliny the Younger refer to a group called "Christians,"[148] which evidences a group sharing common traits as early as AD 64.
- By the end of the second century, these Christian communities and their respective leaders held the four gospels and many of Paul's writings in high regard. These eventually found their way into the formalized collection of New Testament writings.

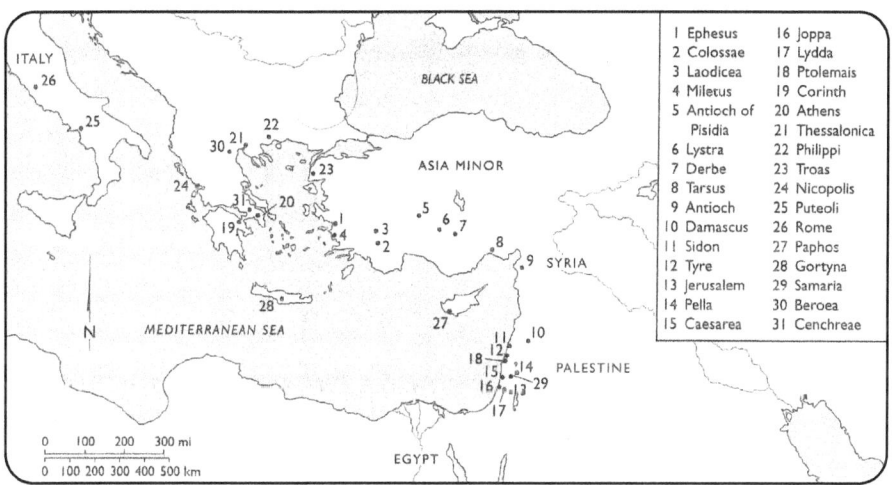

Figure 17. Christian communities between AD 70 and 100
Credit: W.H.C. Frend. Darton, Longman and Todd. Used with permission.

Formal Arrangement of the New Testament

So how was it that some of these writings came to be "selected" for inclusion into the eventual New Testament? I think Lee McDonald says it well: The corridors of research are "dimly lit" in this particular area.[149] However, that is not to say that we cannot derive any fruit from our investigations here. There are data points to consider that, in my opinion, lead to an account of what likely took place.

The prominent early church fathers Irenaeus of Lyon, Clement of Alexandria,

Tertullian of Carthage, and Eusebius of Caesarea begin to paint a picture for us of the emerging package of New Testament writings. On the following page is a table outlining which texts they referenced or alluded to in their respective writings.

Please note that in relation to the data in Table 5, Eusebius is the only one to clearly designate those texts as identifiable and authoritative Scripture. The lists generated from the other fathers are those writings we can be reasonably confident that they held in good esteem as a minimum standard.

This data potentially tells us that there was something of a universal agreement on which Christian writings were valued across time and the geography of the wider Mediterranean. Of the twenty-seven books that would eventually make their way into the New Testament collection, these fathers all likely agreed on the validity of over two-thirds of the documents. There appeared to be an unshakable valuing of the four gospels accompanied by a near-consistent revering of the apostle Paul's writings, with some debate existing around the outskirts.

However, it's worth noting that up until the point of Eusebius there is no evidence of a formal council taking place that would "officially" authorize a final collection of New Testament documents.[150] The first "universal" council of the church took place in Nicaea under the reign of Emperor Constantine in AD 325.[151] With the exception of the supposed death and resurrection of Christ, the reign of Constantine is arguably the most impactful moment in the history of the Christian faith.

Table 5: Early Church Fathers and the Texts They Considered[152]

	Early Church Father	Irenaeus	Clement	Tertullian	Eusebius
	Estimated Date	AD 170 - 180	AD 150 - 215	AD 160 - 225	AD 320 - 342
Writings That Would Eventually Make Up the New Testament	Matthew	x	x	x	x
	Mark	x	x	x	x
	Luke	x	x	x	x
	John	x	x	x	x
	1 Peter	x	x	x	x
	1 John	x	x	x	x
	Romans	x	x	x	x
	1 Corinthians	x	x	x	x
	2 Corinthians	x	x	x	x
	Galatians	x	x	x	x
	Ephesians	x	x	x	x
	Philippians	x	x	x	x
	Colossians	x	x	x	x
	1 Thessalonians	x	x	x	x
	2 Thessalonians	x	x	x	x
	1 Timothy	x	x	x	x
	2 Timothy	x	x	x	x
	Titus	x	x	x	x
	Revelation	x	x	x	x
	Acts			x	x
	James				
	2 Peter				
	2 John	x	x		
	3 John	x			
	Jude		x	x	
	Hebrews		x		x
	Philemon		x	x	x

Table 5, continued

	Early Church Father	Irenaeus	Clement	Tertullian	Eusebius
	Estimated Date	AD 170 - 180	AD 150 - 215	AD 160 - 225	AD 320 - 342
Writings That Would Eventually Be Excluded from the New Testament Collection	Shepherd of Hermas	x	x		
	1 Clement	x	x		
	Barnabas		x		
	Preaching of Peter		x		
	Sibylline Oracles		x		
	Didache		x		
	Gospel of Hebrews		x		
	Gospel of Egyptians		x		
	Tradition of Matthias		x		

Constantine and the Council of Nicaea

The hugely popular fictional novel *The Da Vinci Code* puts forward the idea that the Roman Emperor Constantine created the Christian Bible that we know today so he could solidify his power base in the Roman Empire through the unification of Roman society under the one religion.[153] The book propagates the idea that the ignition point of this supposed consolidation of power was the Council of Nicaea in AD 325.[154] The book was hugely popular and many people have walked away suspecting that the above conspiracy theory is more likely to be true than false. Does this match up with the evidence?

A proper understanding of the Council of Nicaea can only be obtained by examining its preceding context: the reign of Emperor Diocletian and Constantine's rise to power. Up until this moment, the Christian movement was a minority in the empire, occupying some 5 to 8 percent of the population. In AD 303, Diocletian inaugurated an empire-wide persecution of the Christians, which involved the burning of Christian books, demolition of Christian churches, removal of class privileges, eventual imprisonment of high-ranking Christian clergy, and execution of Christians for not performing cultural pagan sacrifices. This period of persecution lasted for nearly a decade.[155]

Why the persecution? Well, ever since the birth of Christianity, there was persecution of its followers to varying degrees. Initially it was carried out by the Jews, but as time went on the role of chief persecutor was taken by the Roman pagans and their administrative officials. Pagans believed that the gods provided the necessities of life: health, prosperity, fertility, and so on. Worship was performed to these gods through prayer and animal sacrifices. If a plague, famine, drought, or earthquake struck a community, it was because the gods were angry that they didn't receive the appropriate worship from the relevant members of that community. When these events occurred, the minority Christians would incur wrath from their pagan counterparts because they worshipped the one true Jesus, which ultimately must have provoked the pagan gods.[156]

Emperor Diocletian voluntarily abdicated in AD 305 and was replaced by Constantine. Fast forward to the famous battle at Milvian Bridge (AD 312), and Constantine supposedly underwent something of a miraculous conversion to Christianity. He then won this battle resoundingly against his opponent Maxentius, establishing himself as the senior emperor of the western Roman Empire all at the ripe old age of thirty-two.[157]

The eastern Roman Empire was ruled by Licinius; he and Constantine met in Milan in AD 313. It was here that a policy was agreed upon for freedom for all religions including paganism and Christianity. For the first time, the Roman Empire gave Christianity full legal status as an officially tolerated faith.[158]

Licinius, however, was still a pagan ruler, and he grew increasingly anti-Christian over the next decade. In AD 320, he upped the ante and started a violent persecution of Christians, which involved the destruction of church buildings and execution of bishops and presbyters (church leaders).

Tensions built between the pro-Christian Constantine and Licinius, which led to war in AD 324. Constantine won and became the undisputed master of the entire Roman Empire.[159]

Now that Constantine held total control, he devoted his full attention to unifying the empire. In AD 325, Constantine summoned the first universal council of church leadership from all across the Mediterranean to Nicaea in northwest Asia Minor to settle the greatest theological dispute to ever impact the Christian faith: the Arian controversy.[160] In short, the debate focused upon the precise nature of Jesus's divinity. Was Jesus fully God, fully human, or some other combination of both? The debate was causing much division through the church across the Mediterranean, and Constantine—wanting a unified empire—sought to bring it to a head at Nicaea.

The outputs of the Council of Nicaea were the following:

1. The Nicene Creed

A universally agreed upon confession of faith (doctrinal statement), which sought to address the Arian controversy:

> We believe in one God, the Father almighty, Creator of all things visible and invisible; and in one Lord Jesus Christ, the Son of God, begotten of the Father, only-begotten, that is, from the essence of the Father, God from God, light from light, true God from true God, begotten, not created, of the same essence as the Father, through Whom [i.e., through Christ] all things were created both in heaven and on earth; Who for us human beings and for our salvation came down and was incarnate, was made man, suffered and rose again on the third day, ascended into heaven, and is coming again to judge the living and the dead; and [we believe] in the Holy Spirit.[161]

2. Structural implementations

The council enacted several initiatives to give the church structure, delineate responsibilities, and improve communication among the churches.[162]

Sir Leigh Teabing, the fictional British Royal Historian in *The Da Vinci Code*, loosely implies that it was at or around the Council of Nicaea where

Constantine created the Christian Bible.[163] In reality, however, there is no evidence that this took place. What we do have evidence for is Constantine's instruction to the Bishop Eusebius of Caesarea in AD 331 to print fifty copies of the sacred Scriptures for churches that were being built in his imperial city, Constantinople:[164]

> Victor Constantinus, Maximus Augustus, to Eusebius.
>
> It happens, through the favoring providence of God our Savior, that great numbers have united themselves to the most holy church in the city which is called by my name. It seems, therefore, highly requisite, since that city is rapidly advancing in prosperity in all other respects, that the number of churches should also be increased. Do you, therefore, receive with all readiness my determination on this behalf. I have thought it expedient to instruct your Prudence to order fifty copies of the sacred scriptures (the provision and use of which you know to be most needful for the instruction of the Church) to be written on a prepared parchment in a legible manner, and in a commodious and portable form, by transcribers thoroughly practiced in their art.[165]

As we have discussed earlier in this chapter, an agreed corpus of Christian writings likely already existed in the second and third centuries. Thus, it is more than likely that Constantine instructed Eusebius here to print a pre-existing collection of Scripture rather than create a new Bible. The text above certainly conveys such. We have evidence of Constantine extending religious freedoms, getting involved in a church dispute, and requesting the printing of sacred Scripture. The creation of an alternative Bible, however, is entirely without foundation.

What *The Da Vinci Code* may get somewhat right, however, is the suggestion that Constantine's Christian conversion may not have been genuine. This area remains a consistent subject of debate among historians today.[166] It is beyond dispute that the conversion of Constantine, sincere or otherwise, was one of the most significant events in the history of Western civilization. It sparked the transition of Christianity from a persecuted and hated minority religion to the majority religion of the Roman Empire by the end of the fourth century. All emperors after Constantine, with only one exception, were Christian.[167]

When Does the New Testament Finally Settle?

The first list that contains all of the books in our modern day New Testament appears to be that of Athanasius of Alexandria in AD 367. The collection he listed would ultimately prevail in the majority of churches in succeeding centuries.[168]

However, in all probability the primary reason for this prevailing collection is owed to the work undertaken by Jerome from AD 383 to 405 when he translated this twenty-seven book collection into Latin at the request of Pope Damasus.[169] Latin was the first language of the western Roman Empire,[170] and the Vulgate became the official Bible of the medieval church for a period spanning over one thousand years.[171] This would change at the Council of Trent in 1546, when the Catholic church chose to incorporate new books into its Old Testament (see Appendix 3); however, the New Testament would remain unchanged.

Gnostic Gospels and Other Texts

As fictional as *The Da Vinci Code* is, it does reference the Gnostic gospels, which are real. Were these gospels and other texts reservoirs of alternative truth that were hidden and suppressed by the church?

The adjacent table outlines a selection of these supposed other gospels and texts that have been found to date (see Appendix 6 for a full listing):

Table 6: Gnostic Gospels

Material	Estimated Date of Authorship	Description
Infancy Gospel of Thomas	Somewhere between 1st and 6th century[172]	A collection of stories centered upon Jesus's childhood and his miracle-working abilities. Many of the accounts do not portray Jesus in a favorable light; for example, he uses his supernatural powers to kill off playmates who irritate him and humiliates teachers who discipline him.[173]
The Proto-Gospel of James	Late 2nd century[174]	An account of the events leading up to and immediately following the birth of Jesus with the primary focus on Jesus's mother Mary's upbringing, young life, and engagement to Joseph.[175]
The Gospel of the Nazarenes	Mid 2nd century[176]	Contains accounts of Jesus's baptism, teaching, healing, and death. The gospel enjoyed a long life with sources attesting to it from the late 2nd to the 13th century.[177]
The Gospel of the Ebionites	Mid to late 2nd century[178]	A gospel account that conflates the gospels of Matthew, Mark, and Luke. It covers Jesus's baptism, his call of the twelve, his public ministry, the Last Supper, and his death.[179]
The Gospel according to the Hebrews	Early to mid 2nd century[180]	In a similar manner to the Gospel of the Nazarenes, this gospel is a narrative account of Jesus's entire public ministry, from beginning to end, including his resurrection. This gospel was known and used in Egypt.[181]

Material	Estimated Date of Authorship	Description
A Gospel Harmony: The Diatessaron	AD 160 to 170[182]	The first harmonization of the four biblical gospels combined with other gospel traditions,[183] authored by the Christian philosopher and theologian Tatian.[184] Diatessaron means "through the four."[185]
The Gospel according to Thomas	AD 100 to 150[186]	This gospel is the most widely known, most studied, and most controversial of all the supposed gospels outside the New Testament. A fully copy of the gospel in Coptic was discovered in the Nag Hammadi library in 1945. Comprised entirely of sayings attributed to Jesus, there is no mention of his supposed miracles, death, or resurrection (discussed further below).[187]
The Gospel of Peter	Early to mid 2nd century[188]	A gospel that provides an alternative version of the death and resurrection of Jesus. The writing is similar in many respects to the biblical gospels, but its most striking difference pertains to its account of Jesus exiting the tomb. He emerges as tall as a mountain, with the cross trailing behind him and Jesus declaring that the message of salvation has been proclaimed in the realm of the dead.[189]
The Gospel of Judas	AD 140 to 150[190]	This gospel contains a series of dialogues between Jesus and his disciples during the Passover week prior to his crucifixion. In these conversations, Jesus reveals the hidden truths of salvation to his disciples, especially Judas. There is no mention of his supposed death and resurrection.[191]
The Gospel of Philip	3rd century[192]	A collection of disparate Gnostic mystical reflections, supposedly recorded by Jesus's disciple Philip. We have one manuscript of this gospel that was discovered at Nag Hammadi, and it possibly alludes to the nature of the relationship Jesus held with Mary Magdalene. However, due to the incomplete nature of the manuscript, we cannot determine what this supposed relationship was.[193]

As mentioned above, the most critically examined "alternative gospel" of all these texts is the Gospel according to Thomas. The text is controversial because there is no mention of miracles, the death of Jesus, or his resurrection. The text does not stress the importance of Jesus's human death and resurrection for salvation. The gospel proposes that salvation comes not by believing in Christ's death and resurrection, but rather by interpreting his sayings.[194]

Given this and the other alternative texts listed above, should the accuracy of the traditional New Testament gospel accounts be doubted? I think not for a couple of reasons.

First, we have some problems with the dating of the alternative texts. Leigh Teabing in *The Da Vinci Code* refers to these texts as being "the earliest Christian records." He then refers to the Gospel of Philip,[195] which is estimated to have been written in the third century AD, some 150 to 200 years after the writing of the New Testament documents. As you can see from the above data in the table, most of these alternative texts were written a very long time after the events they are purporting to relay. If the supposed gap of the New Testament writings is a problem for you, then these texts definitely won't pass that test either.

However, assuming that the late date of authorship isn't an insurmountable problem (as it hasn't been for many in establishing ancient history), do any of these texts present a challenge to the New Testament writings? Clearly, yes, they do. Some present an alternative worldview to the Christian faith, and none of us can sit here and say definitively that they are untrue. However, we are trying to do history here, and doing history is about weighing probabilities on the basis of evidence and determining what is most likely to have occurred.

Contrary to Leigh Teabing's thesis, there is no evidence that alternative gospel texts were suppressed and hidden by an organized church or authority at any point in history. To believe such a thesis (which I have seen an alarming number of people do) is, in my opinion, to make a blind leap of faith that is not rooted in any form of evidence. I think the more realistic and somewhat dull reality here is that these Gnostic texts were out there in the open but had a very limited recognition because they were written much later than other New Testament documents and were generally regarded as untruthful.

Contradictions in the New Testament

Many argue that the New Testament, and the broader Bible for that matter, are unreliable as historical documents because they contain internal contradictions. For instance, none of the four gospels agree on what was written above the head of Jesus during his crucifixion:

Matthew 27:37	Above his head they placed the written charge against him: THIS IS JESUS, THE KING OF THE JEWS.
Mark 15:26	The written notice of the charge against him read: THE KING OF THE JEWS.
Luke 23:38	There was a written notice above him, which read: THIS IS THE KING OF THE JEWS.
John 19:19	Pilate had a notice prepared and fastened to the cross. It read: JESUS OF NAZARETH, THE KING OF THE JEWS.

And there are seemingly two differing accounts of how Judas died:

Matthew 27:5	So Judas threw the money into the temple and left. Then he went away and hanged himself.
Acts 1:18	With the payment he received for his wickedness, Judas bought a field; there he fell headlong, his body burst open and all his intestines spilled out.

There are two different genealogies of Jesus contained in Matthew 1:1–17 and Luke 3:23–38. There are many other contradictions in the Bible that, if we were to discuss them, could make up an entirely new book. However, does the existence of multiple contradictions materially affect the credibility of the Bible to communicate historical events?

In my opinion, no. As previously discussed in this chapter, the New Testament is filled with writings that were written some thirty to fifty years after the events they reported on. It should hardly be surprising that some of the accounts will differ on various details. Some would protest, however, that if we can't get the details right on the little things, then how could we get them right on the bigger things (e.g., Jesus's supposed resurrection)?

My beloved West Coast Eagles (an Australian rules football team) won their inaugural title back in 1992. My fellow supporters and I frequently reminisce about that memorable day some thirty years ago. It won't be surprising that we often have differing recollections about who did and didn't play well, the score at halftime, and who did the pre-game entertainment. However, we always agree, without fail, that the Eagles won that day.

To argue that the New Testament authors couldn't arrive at a resurrection narrative without getting all the other details right is akin to saying that us Eagles fans forgot who won the match because we disagreed on the exact score. To place these sorts of expectations upon the people relaying the events and the texts themselves is to me unrealistic and unfair. At the end of the day, the New Testament is very consistent and uniform in that it conveys an account of Jesus crucified and resurrected. There is no ambiguity on that point.

Things That Support the Authenticity of the New Testament

Are there any other elements in the New Testament writings that help us assess their truthfulness? There are two additional things that can be said here:

1. The New Testament is not self-serving

The gospel accounts do not paint the disciples in a fantastic light. They frequently misunderstand Jesus, and they quarrel with one another. They seemingly abandon Jesus at his death, and on the whole, they're not portrayed as capable, intelligent people who will be likely to change the ideological landscape of the Western world. If you were seeking to concoct a story to garner credibility to create a world religion, then the gospel accounts would probably not be your best leading material. As such, this lends support to the text's authenticity rather than it having a spurious nature.

2. The details in the New Testament line up with historical evidence

Details pertaining to geography, botany, local customs, and names common to the region all seem to be on the money in the New Testament when compared to the external evidence.[196] Bart Ehrman in his debate with Peter Williams on this very point says that details such as these have "no bearing on the question" of whether Jesus did what is recorded in the New Testament.[197] But surely they have some bearing? If we were evaluating two historical accounts and one had all the incidental details right and the other had all those details wrong, which one would we be more likely to trust? Of course, getting the incidental details right doesn't prove that the primary account is true, but surely it helps to lend it credibility.

In Summary

I think the totality of the evidence that I have put forward urges us to take the New Testament writings seriously and trust them rather than distrust them. Theories will always abound about their supposedly misleading nature; this theorizing is more rooted in blind faith than evidence. There are no "proofs" or closed arguments in this realm. Some folks speak dogmatically of the New Testament as a pristine, undisturbed reservoir of truth, while others call it a concoction of mankind to manipulate the masses. All these people ignore a swathe of history and evidence that paints a far more nuanced picture of reality. It appears that God has used human beings to make himself known through the Bible, and it's important that we remember that from time to time so we can have realistic expectations about what we can know and don't know.

v. Still Relevant Today
The Bible Makes Some Startling Claims Regarding the Meaning and Function of the Universe, That, If True, Change the Way We See Everything

In my experience, many people have made the throwaway line that the Bible is obsolete and has no material bearing on modern Western society. Whenever I hear such a claim, I can be reasonably confident that the person has never read the Bible.

The Bible makes thoroughly outlandish claims, which, if true, will affect every nook and cranny of your life. It will influence the way you view yourself. It will influence your career and how you operate within it. It will influence your relationships. It will influence how you drive, how you spend your money, what you wear, etc. Make no mistake, it will invade and pervade every corner of your life.

The question of biblical obsolescence is not one that someone should be asking in the first place. The only question that initially matters is whether it is true. As C. S. Lewis said, "Christianity, if false, is of no importance, and if true, of infinite importance. The one thing it cannot be is moderately important."[198]

In light of all this, I think the Bible is a collection of books that should be taken seriously. In the next chapter I will introduce the person of Jesus, who is the single biggest pillar of Christian belief and who the Bible references in significant detail.

CHAPTER 4

DID JESUS EXIST? WHO WAS HE?

In the last chapter, I put forward the case that the Bible should be taken seriously as a credible historical collection of documents. Without a doubt, the most controversial claims of the Bible pertain to an individual named Jesus whom the entire Christian faith is centered upon. Therefore, it is essential that we probe deeper into the questions of whether Jesus existed and who he was.

Did Jesus Exist?

From my survey, the consistent consensus that the greater majority of serious historians arrive at is that Jesus existed beyond reasonable doubt. This isn't a radical statement. Scholars consistently turn to the *Oxford Classical Dictionary* and the volumes of *Cambridge Ancient History* to ascertain the "lay of the land" of ancient historical matters. These reference works and many others state that Jesus existed.[1]

What sources are drawn upon to confirm Jesus's existence?

1. The New Testament

As discussed in the previous chapter, the New Testament is a collection of twenty-seven books that all refer to Jesus.

2. Tacitus

Outside the Bible, Tacitus is probably the most revered non-biblical source for Jesus. Tacitus was a Roman aristocrat who rose through the ranks to become the proconsul, or head, in the province of Asia, now modern-day Turkey. He had a first-class education and unfettered access to imperial sources.[2]

Tacitus wrote the *Annals*, which recounted the careers of several Roman emperors from AD 14 to 69. He mentioned Jesus in passing when discussing the great fire of Rome in AD 64, which Emperor Nero blamed on the Christians. In his writing, Tacitus confirmed that Jesus existed and that he was executed by Pontius Pilate.[3] He elaborates no further than that.

3. Josephus

Josephus is the world's most famous and influential Jewish historian. He was born in AD 37.[4] He wrote the *Antiquities of the Jews* in AD 95, which is a twenty-volume work of the history of the Jewish people.[5] In this work, there are two references to Jesus, in books 18 and 20.[6]

In book 18, Josephus wrote:

> About this time there lived Jesus, a wise man, *if indeed one ought to call him a man*. For he was one who wrought surprising feats and was a teacher of such people as accept the truth gladly. He won over many Jews and many of the Greeks. *He was the Messiah*. When Pilate, upon hearing him accused by men of the highest standing amongst us, had condemned him to be crucified, those who had in the first place come to love him did not give up their affection for him. *On the third day he appeared to them restored to life, for the prophets of God had prophesied these and countless other marvelous things about him*. And the tribe of the Christians, so called after him, has still to this day not disappeared.[7]

The overwhelming judgment of scholars today is that the italicized parts above are Christian embellishments on Josephus's original work. Josephus was not a Christian, and these statements simply do not make sense in light of the rest of his writing and what we know of his character.[8] That said, the majority of scholars seem to be comfortable saying the rest of the text is authentic, which has Josephus confirming the existence of Jesus and his subsequent crucifixion.

The book 20 reference is far less controversial; Josephus wrote about the death of Jesus's brother James:

> And so he [Ananus the high priest] convened the judges of the Sanhedrin and brought before them a man named James, the brother of Jesus who was called the Christ, and certain others. He accused them of having transgressed the law and delivered them up to be stoned. Those of the inhabitants of the city who were considered the most fair-minded and who were strict in observance of the law were offended at this.[9]

In summary, here we have a Jewish historian who seems to have suffered from some later embellishment but at the core confirmed the existence and execution of Jesus.

Other Sources

There are other sources that are of some value to exploring the historical Jesus, namely, Suetonius, Pliny the Younger, Lucian, Thallus, Celsus, and Mara Serapion. However, each of these sources have limitations that make them hard to rely upon for concrete information about Jesus.[10]

Are There Really Enough Sources Here?

A lot of skeptics will say that we only have two "independent" sources for the historical Jesus, which is nowhere near sufficient. To call texts "independent" is a misnomer and the presumption that somehow these independent sources are to be trusted more than "dependent" sources is, in my opinion, flawed thinking. However, in the interest of setting a really high bar here, I will indulge in the premise for a moment.

The logical question to ask at this point is how many sources do we have for other comparable historical figures?

Table 7: Historical Figures and Their Sources

Historical Figure	Key Literary Sources
Julius Caesar	• Julius Caesar – Gallic Wars • Cicero • Sallust – Catiline • Suetonius – Divus Julius • Plutarch – Caesar • Appian – Civil Wars • Cassius Dio – History[11]
Socrates	• Aristophanes – Nubes • Plato • Xenophon – Memorabilia, Apologia Socrates, Symposium, Oeconomicus • Aeschines of Sphettus • Antisthenes • Aristotle – Metaphysica, Ethica Nicomachea, Magna Moralia[12]
Alexander the Great	• Arrian • Strabo • Curtius Rufus • Diodorus Siculus – book 17 • Justin – books 11–12 • Metz Epitome[13]
Cleopatra	• Plutarch – Life of Antony • Cassius Dio – History • Josephus – The Jewish War, Jewish Antiquities • Cicero – Letters to Atticus • Horace – Odes and Epodes[14]

As you can see, there isn't an embarrassment of riches here for source material for major figures of a similar period. Now, obviously, the literary evidence isn't the only factor at play here; I understand that there are other streams of evidence that need to be evaluated in conjunction with the literary material. The point that I want to make, however, is that when people question the historicity of Jesus based upon the number of sources, they seem to nearly always do so without a good knowledge of how other figures look in comparison. Inevitably, what I find after further exploration is that these people are actually after more evidence and sources than Jesus's contemporaries because the claims of Jesus are so extraordinary that they require extraordinary evidence.

Do Extraordinary Claims Require Extraordinary Evidence?

It's a nice quip, and it feels true at first hearing. For sure, we yearn for extraordinary evidence in the face of extraordinary claims. I, like many of my readers, would love it if video footage existed of Jesus rising from the dead.

If video evidence of Jesus resurrecting is what you require to accept the resurrection as a historical reality, then okay. Everyone has a different standard and lens that they apply to these matters, and I think herein lies the challenge with the quip. The quip is stated dogmatically, but it really does depend upon the eye of the beholder. What is extraordinary evidence to some is not to others.

For those people who do require a high level of "extraordinary evidence," I am concerned that this may limit their ability to objectively review evidence. If one is closed in their initial stance, does this inhibit their ability to be persuaded by the available evidence that might convince them if they evaluated things in a more open manner? It seems to me that a more reasoned and rational way to evaluate extraordinary claims is to evaluate the evidence that we should reasonably and rationally expect to find if that claim were true. Perhaps then, if we let the evidence "marinate," we might arrive at a different position than if we remained closed off from the start.

As the late great comedian Norm Macdonald reminded us, one must *choose* to become a Christian.[15] Despite what some Christians teach, the case for Christianity is not so compelling that all personal doubt is fully absolved. All people must be careful not to set themselves an impossibly high bar for belief that ultimately prevents them from ascertaining truth on any level.

Who Was Jesus?

Art of the post-Jesus era depicts him as a sacrificial lamb, meek, weak even, an undeserving victim who carried the weight of the world on his shoulders. The Bible certainly does communicate elements of his character to this effect; however, it is inaccurate to characterize Jesus purely in those terms. When you take a closer look at the Bible and truly study it properly, you will find that Jesus was a pretty disruptive and revolutionary individual. He looked at things differently, and he didn't conform to others' expectations. He was hard to pigeonhole, and it seems from the biblical texts that he had a consistent track record of surprising people. One day Jesus is telling an adulterer that her sins are pardoned,[16] and another day he is chastising the Pharisees (religious "gurus" of the day) for their insincere religious practices.[17] Another day he tells people to love their enemies,[18] then later he says that he has come to divide and pit brother against brother, son against father, and so forth.[19] Does this make Jesus inconsistent? I'd say no, but it certainly makes him intriguing.

Early Life and Upbringing

According to Christian tradition, Jesus was born in Bethlehem, Judea[20] around the year 4 BC[21] (for further commentary on why Jesus was born BC, please see footnote reference).[22] From there, he and his parents escaped King Herod the Great's mass infant execution and headed to Egypt.[23] Not long after that Herod died, and Jesus's family eventually settled in the region of Nazareth. Jesus grew up there and he most likely became a carpenter, following in his father's footsteps as was customary in that culture.[24] In that time Nazareth was a village of no more than four hundred people, and it was not regarded as significant by ancient Jewish historians. Most people would probably have been engaged in agriculture or other minor industries, and the village could have provided Joseph and his family with enough work (with some trips to neighboring villages to supplement their living). In terms of social status, there is some debate on where Jesus's family sat on the societal spectrum. Some say they were poorer than peasants but richer than beggars. Others argue that the family was relatively well-off and that carpenters were actually looked up to in that society.[25] Either way, there is no indication in the Bible or any other source of Jesus's precise financial status, and such speculation can be never-ending. In the end, it seems more likely that the family was neither poor nor extremely wealthy given their area of residence.

In terms of Jesus's education, significant New Testament scholars believe that Jesus could at least read; however, given the educational standards of the day, his literacy level would have been extremely basic. Jesus's first language would have been Aramaic (the language of Palestine and the surrounding area), and he may have also known some Hebrew (the language of the ancient Scriptures) and perhaps some Greek also.[26]

The question of whether Jesus was married became prominent in the mid-2000s with the release of *The Da Vinci Code*, which suggested that Jesus had married Mary Magdalene and the church had subsequently covered it up. It would have been very unusual for a Jewish man like Jesus to remain unmarried well into his thirties in that society. The biblical command from Genesis 1:22 to "be fruitful and multiply" was taken seriously. However, there is no evidence to suggest that Jesus was married. The early church would have had no reason to suppress Jesus's marriage, so it should remain the position that Jesus was an unmarried man.[27]

Jesus grew up in a Jewish family; he would have been well-versed in the story of Israel, Jewish customs, and the Hebrew Scriptures from a young age. However, it must be noted that first century Judaism was extremely diverse, and there were many ways of being Jewish. This can be seen in the heated debates that Jesus had with other Jewish thinkers in his time of ministry pertaining to what it really meant to be a Jew in belief and practice.[28]

The Ministry Period

There is some debate on how long Jesus's public ministry lasted. Some say it was one year, whereas others suggest it was more likely a period of several years.[29] Either way, with a lot of these dating issues it is hard to know precisely, but most scholars agree that Jesus's public ministry commenced with his baptism by John the Baptist in the river Jordan[30] around AD 28.[31]

Following his baptism, Jesus traveled around the villages of Galilee announcing a message that included:

- Summoning people to repent
- Announcing the kingdom, or reign, of Israel's God through the use of parables (stories)

To enact this message, Jesus performed remarkable cures or "miracles" and he interacted with a very socioculturally diverse group. He had twelve disciples who traveled with him and observed him up close.[32]

Even though Jesus seemingly did good works in the community, he upset the Jewish leadership and establishment seemingly right from the beginning. Jesus was an irregular, and even though he had presented as a Rabbi, he had not entered by the right door or climbed the right ladder. He was judged by these leaders for fraternizing with disreputable people and not obeying other traditional Jewish customs. In probably his greatest insult to them, Jesus called them hypocrites and accused them of caring more about their own status than the hearts of people. In doing this, Jesus undermined their authority. Ultimately, Jesus claimed to be equal with God, and with that the Jewish leaders had their smoking gun. Now they could get rid of the heretic and restore order to their power base.[33]

These activities, and especially one dramatic action in the temple, incurred the wrath of some Jewish believers, notably of the high priestly establishment. Partly because of this, Jesus was handed over to the Roman authorities and executed in a style regularly used for insurrectionists. Not long after this, Jesus's followers claimed that he had been raised from the dead.[34]

We are on relatively safe ground to say that Jesus has been the most significant and influential individual to have ever walked on planet earth. But how do we account for his fame? The consensus conclusion of modern Western society is that Jesus didn't rise from the dead and that there are other more rational and likely explanations to account for his fame and significance. We will explore these other explanations in the next chapter.

CHAPTER 5

JESUS IS FAMOUS BECAUSE...

It's one thing to say that Jesus existed, but it's another matter entirely to conclude that he rose from the dead. Anyone hearing this claim for the first time would presume that this surely didn't happen and that there must be some alternative explanation for how and why such a belief propagated. We'll now explore these alternate theories and their viability.

Theory 1: Game of Telephone

Jesus and his supposed religion are simply a product of progressive storytelling. The claimed miracles and resurrection are just legend; these are greatly exaggerated claims that have evolved over the years.

The skeptic Bart Ehrman says the following:

> It is [oral circulation] that causes special problems for historians who want to know what actually happened in the life of Jesus. We don't have any written records from his own day, only later accounts written by people who had heard the stories that had been in circulation for so many years. What happens, though, to stories as they circulate by word of mouth? Did you, or your kids, ever play the party game telephone? Kids all sit in a circle, one kid whispers a story to the one sitting next to her, who tells it to the one next to her, and so on, around the circle, until it comes back to the first kid—and by then it's a different story. (If it weren't a different story every time, it would be a pretty pointless game to play.)[1]

Craig Blomberg puts forward the following alternative view:

> When you're carefully memorizing something and taking care not to pass it along until you're sure you've got it right, you're doing something very different from playing the game of telephone. In telephone half of the fun is that the person may not have got it right or even heard it right the first time, and they cannot ask the person to repeat it. Then you immediately pass it along, also in whispered tones that make it more likely the next person will goof something up even more. So yes, by the time it has circulated through a room of thirty people, the results can be hilarious.[2]

Then we should ask: Why isn't the telephone game a good analogy to describe passing along ancient oral traditions? Blomberg responds:

> If you really wanted to develop that analogy in light of the checks and balances of the first-century community, you'd have to say that every third person out loud in a very clear voice, would have to ask the first person, "Do I still have it right?" and change if he didn't. The community would constantly be monitoring what was said and intervening to make corrections along the way. That would preserve the integrity of the message. And the result would be very different from that of a childish game of telephone.[3]

To bring Blomberg's view to the fore, let's examine the world of the disciples after the supposed resurrection of Jesus. Fifty days after the event, Peter delivers a speech to the public in Jerusalem that results in the conversion of approximately three thousand people. From here the fuse is lit and the early Christian faith is at serious loggerheads with the established Jewish order. Followers of Jesus are persecuted heavily in the region by the Jewish leaders, which ultimately results in their geographical spreading as a people; thus, the Christian faith spreads at a rapid rate throughout the Mediterranean world.

Blomberg alludes to the oral tradition that was prevalent in the first century and previous Jewish culture. In a nutshell, the Jews took oral tradition very seriously. As I discussed earlier in chapter 3, instantaneous written communication was not prevalent in this culture. This culture heavily relied on oral transmission to communicate because literacy rates were very low. If errors were made, there were much more serious consequences in their everyday affairs than there would be in our culture. As such, they must have been very careful to ensure that events and instructions were communicated accurately and thoroughly.

In light of this, is it likely that this culture miscommunicated Jesus's death to be a resurrection at some point in the oral transfer? Given that this new Christian worldview was in direct opposition to the ruling authorities and any subscription would likely result in direct persecution, I personally think it more likely that they would have been incredibly scrupulous in ascertaining what transpired. As such, I think this theory has little credibility in explaining the potential origins of a supposed resurrection narrative.

Theory 2: It's a Myth Purposefully Created

Personally, I find this the hardest theory to stomach regarding Jesus's fame. It became popular again in 2005 when Dan Brown published *The Da Vinci Code*, which portrayed a secretive and dark religious organization that sought to manipulate Christianity's teachings to its own advantage. The book and subsequent movie came and went, but this theory is raised with me from time to time.

When it is raised, I ask for the proponent to provide evidence for its existence—none ever comes. No doubt the message of Christianity has been misconstrued in times of history (e.g., the Crusades), but that is not what we're talking about here. We are talking about the emergence of Christianity, and there is no evidence to suggest that its origins had a motivation of self-gain or power enhancement. Nearly all of the disciples were likely martyred as very poor people.

Theory 3: He Didn't Really Die (The Swoon Theory)

The swoon theory proposes that Jesus didn't really die on the cross; rather he just severely fainted, and subsequently his health improved dramatically.

Later his disciples mistook his resuscitation for resurrection. To consider this theory, we need to understand what a Roman crucifixion looked like.

In all likelihood, the Romans adopted the crucifixion process from the Carthaginians. The process would typically involve an initial flogging followed by the victim carrying the wooden beam to the place of execution where he or she was nailed to it with outstretched arms, raised up, and seated on a small wooden peg. The form of execution would vary, as the executioners were given full rein to do as they willed. In the ancient world, crucifixion was an utterly offensive affair.[4] It was very labor, time, and visually intensive. It was probably intended that way to inflict as much pain and embarrassment on its victims as possible and act as a deterrent to public witnesses who might have dared challenge the will of Rome. The pain delivered via crucifixion was so intense that they invented a new word to describe it, "excruciating," which means "out of the cross."[5]

The odds of surviving a crucifixion were incredibly low at best. In the absence of modern medicine, it would take staggering faith to think that Jesus didn't die on the cross and simply recovered. If that were the case, then surely the Romans would have rearrested him and had another crack. There is no evidence of that occurring, and on the whole, I think it nearly impossible that the Swoon Theory has any chance of being true.

Theory 4: It Was All a Hoax

The hoax theory contains several possibilities. First, I will consider the replacement theory, which comes in two forms.

The first form says that Jesus wasn't crucified; rather a last-minute lookalike stood in for him, thus explaining why Jesus was able to portray himself as subsequently resurrected.

The second form says that Jesus was crucified; however, a twin brother or lookalike took his place following the crucifixion so that it appeared he had resurrected.

I think these theories are unlikely for the following reasons:

1. If true, these actions are almost more miraculous than a purported resurrection itself. The evidence suggests that Jesus was a seriously well-known and public individual. The idea that someone could stand in for him, or that he had a secret twin brother who was never seen previously in conjunction with him, makes this theory highly unlikely.
2. Why would the disciples or anyone concoct such a plan? If true, this means that the disciples and other Jesus followers falsified his resurrection, created a false faith, and subsequently were killed for believing that faith. Is that really likely?

For these reasons, I think this theory is highly implausible.

Theory 5: Jesus Did Perform Miracles and Rise from the Dead

After reflecting on the above theories and finding them to be unconvincing, I am left with the theory that maybe things happened as the texts say they happened. The apostle Paul (a father of the Christian faith) was self-aware enough to recognize that belief in the resurrection of Jesus Christ could be seen as foolishness.[6] Even when one considers the improbability of the previous theories holding water, to then arrive at a place where Jesus actually did what it is claimed he did still requires a massive leap, which is and should be hard for us to make. It would seem prudent at this stage to not make that leap yet. Rather, I think one needs to take a closer look at the miracles to see whether there is a way to make some sort of sense of the seemingly ridiculous and outrageous.

CHAPTER 6

WHAT DO THE MIRACLES MEAN?

In the previous chapter, I concluded that the last theory standing for the explanation of Jesus's widespread fame was that he actually performed miracles, including his own resurrection. If Jesus did do all these things, what do they mean, and do they matter?

In order to answer these questions properly, we need to understand the backstory that preceded Jesus, specifically the Jewish worldview.

We'll start at the very beginning.

Phase 1: Creation

God created the heavens, the universe, and all manner of life. God created human beings as discrete creatures who are significantly differentiated from other living things. They are differentiated in that they are created "in the image" of God. This means many things, but at an essential level, the human race has a capacity to relate to and communicate with God, which is distinct from other creatures. God intended that humanity would flourish across the planet and live according to his ways and purposes. However, something goes terribly wrong.

Phase 2: The Fall

In the well-trodden story of Adam and Eve, we see human beings deciding to follow their own path and ideals. This triggers a corruption that permeates the entirety of God's creation. Things are not the same from now on, and human beings must contend with the thorns and thistles of life. However, God has a plan...

Phase 3: The Call

There's a guy called Abram who is living in this corrupt and tricky world, and one day God shows up and tells him to go to a new land where he will turn Abram and his people into a great nation.[1] Okay, so Abraham does exactly that.[2] There are plenty of offspring and descendants, and—to cut a long story short—the extended family (who we will now call the Hebrew people) finds itself enslaved to the rulers of Egypt.

Phase 4: Slavery

As the name would indicate, this wasn't a great period on the whole. The Hebrew people believed they were called by the one true God to be a great and prosperous nation. Clearly, it wasn't going to plan until God raised up Moses to deliver them into freedom. Lots of pretty spectacular miracles then took place to facilitate what is, even today, one of the great pillars of Jewish identity.

Phase 5: The Exodus

Most of us know the story. The waters are parted and the Hebrew people escape from their Egyptian captors. God then creates a covenant, or an agreement, with Moses and the Hebrew people, often called the Mosaic Covenant. This covenant included the Ten Commandments, the sacrificial system, and other instructions for the Hebrew people to follow in order to live a whole and prosperous existence. For forty years, the Hebrew people wander the desert, seeking to enter the "promised land," which had been originally promised to Abraham and his descendants.

Phase 6: Settlement

Moses died just prior to the conquest of Jericho, which signaled the fulfillment of the promise. From here, the Hebrew people began to acquire city after city and eventually form what would be the first kingdom of Israel, with Saul as their king. Saul had a mixed record and was eventually replaced by David, made famous by his slaying of the Philistine Goliath.

Phase 7: The Glory Years

To speak in modern terms, King David is the man. Of all the kings that Israel eventually had (with the exception of one particular individual), David is held up as the gold standard of what a godly king should be. He's not perfect, however, and his successors sadly tend to follow a downward trajectory, which ultimately culminates in the Hebrew people being conquered by the Babylonian Empire around the year 600 BC. And with a sense of history repeating itself, the Hebrew people find themselves in captivity.

Phase 8: Captivity Again

This time the Hebrew people are captive in Babylon, and we see another famous Bible story: Daniel and the lions' den. Then the Persian King Cyrus the Great conquers Babylon and liberates the Jewish people, allowing them to return to their homeland in 537 BC.

Phase 9: The Second Temple Era

The next phase is named the second temple era because a new temple was built following the destruction of King Solomon's temple by the Babylonians in circa 587 BC. Life is back to business somewhat for the Hebrew people, but this time they are officially under the rule of the Persian Empire and not an independent nation. Of course, this won't last forever and Alexander the Great conquers the Persian Empire in 332 BC. You guessed it, that won't last forever, and the emerging Roman Empire takes control around the mid-first century BC. This brings us to...

Phase 10: Jesus

I'm sure at this point you see that the Hebrew people must have been pretty exhausted. Their psychological state must have been thoroughly dazed and perplexed. They believed they were God's chosen people, yet God seemingly wasn't there. All they knew was foreign occupation, dilution of religious culture, and getting by. The promises made to Abraham seemed an eternity ago, and surely the people must have been starting to question whether any of that was really history.

To frustrate matters further, there were these prophets, religious gurus of the period, who claimed to be God's messengers. Through the kingdom period of the Hebrew people, they consistently referred to the king who was to come who would restore the kingdom of Israel to a new glory not seen since that great icon King David. There are some sixty-five references to this so-called coming king in the Old Testament writings, which were written over several centuries.[3]

It is not difficult to imagine a spectrum for the Hebrew person. At one end, were those apathetic ones who were bored of hearing about a so-called Messiah or "rescuer" who would sort it all out. In their minds it was codswallop. At the other end, you'd have the zealots, the true believers. They were desperate for the Messiah to show up, and in their minds he would really "sort it out," and by "sort it out" they meant "take on the imperialist Romans."[4]

So with that foundation laid, do the supposed miracles of Jesus speak to this narrative, and, if so, how?

On Table 8 overleaf I have included all references to Jesus's supposed miracles.

While there are thirty-seven accounts listed there, the actual number of potential miracles is probably closer to thirty-one, as several of the references probably refer to the same miracle.[5] At this stage, I encourage you to read through these accounts for yourselves before you read any further, just to get a sense of how these all played out.

Healings dominate the miracle landscape of Jesus, accounting for over two-thirds of the total. As a result, a lot of Christians paint Jesus as an uber compassionate mobile ambulance service who roamed the countryside, doing good wherever he saw the need. However, this isn't an entirely accurate portrayal of Jesus based on the totality of the biblical account. In some instances, he couldn't perform miracles,[6] was resistant to perform them,[7] or just flat out refused.[8] In several cases, Jesus deliberately instructed the beneficiaries of miracles to not tell anyone of the occurrence.[9] It's all rather perplexing.

It seems that the miracles of Jesus were signifying two predominant themes. The first was the undoing of Israel's curse and the second was the ushering in of a new kingdom.

Undoing Israel's Curse

As I referred to earlier, the center of the Jewish worldview focused upon a covenant, or agreement, that existed between God and Israel that was made some 1,300 years before Jesus. God promised to prosper Israel if its people worshipped him and extended justice throughout the world. If they didn't, Israel would experience a variety of agreed-upon nationwide disasters. These included foreign takeover, exile, and a myriad of diseases affecting both the physical and mental state of the people.

Many Jews in the time of Jesus believed that they were living under these covenant curses. The history of Israel is full of some pretty bad times, and the script was seemingly remaining the same. Israel was being ruled by the Romans in the first century and experiencing physical and mental ailments including fever, leprosy, blindness, and demon possession. Many of Jesus's miracles focused upon these specific ailments (see list overleaf).

In summary, it is more than likely that the miracles of Jesus are not some kind of attention-grabbing, "look at me, I have superpowers" thing. Rather they were, in part, a clear signal to the Jewish people that the covenant curses were being lifted, acting as a preview to a new chapter that would eventually be revealed through the fuller work of Jesus.[10]

Table 8: The Miracles of Jesus

Miracle	Gospel Reference
Jesus turns water into wine at the wedding in Cana	John 2:1–11
Jesus heals an official's son at Capernaum in Galilee	John 4:43–54
Jesus drives out an evil spirit from a man in Capernaum	Mark 1:21–27; Luke 4:31–36
Jesus heals Peter's Mother-in-law sick with fever	Matthew 8:14–15; Mark 1:29–31; Luke 4:38–39
Jesus heals many sick and oppressed at evening	Matthew 8:16–17; Mark 1:32–34; Luke 4:40–41
First miraculous catch of fish on the Lake of Gennesaret	Luke 5:1–11
Jesus cleanses a man with leprosy	Matthew 8:1–4; Mark 1:40–45; Luke 5:12–14
Jesus heals a centurion's paralyzed servant in Capernaum	Matthew 8:5–13; Luke 7:1–10
Jesus heals a paralytic who was let down from the roof	Matthew 9:1–8; Mark 2:1–12; Luke 5:17–26
Jesus heals a man's withered hand on the Sabbath	Matthew 12:9–14; Mark 3:1–6; Luke 6:6–11
Jesus raises a widow's son from the dead in Nain	Luke 7:11–17
Jesus calms a storm on the sea	Matthew 8:23–27; Mark 4:35–41; Luke 8:22–25
Jesus casts demons into a herd of pigs	Matthew 8:28–33; Mark 5:1–20; Luke 8:26–39
Jesus heals a woman in the crowd with an issue of blood	Matthew 9:20–22; Mark 5:25–34; Luke 8:42–48
Jesus raises Jairus's daughter back to life	Matthew 9:18, 23–26; Mark 5:21–24, 35–43; Luke 8:40–42, 49–56
Jesus heals two blind men	Matthew 9:27–31
Jesus heals a man who was unable to speak	Matthew 9:32–34
Jesus heals an invalid at Bethesda	John 5:1–15

Miracle	Gospel Reference
Jesus feeds five thousand plus women and children	Matthew 14:13–21; Mark 6:30–44; Luke 9:10–17, John: 6:1–15
Jesus walks on water	Matthew 14:22–33; Mark 6:45–52; John 6:16–21
Jesus heals many sick in Gennesaret as they touch his garment	Matthew 14:34–36; Mark 6:53–56
Jesus heals a gentile woman's demon-possessed daughter	Matthew 15:21–28; Mark 7:24–30
Jesus heals a deaf and mute man	Mark 7:31–37
Jesus feeds four thousand plus women and children	Matthew 15:32–39; Mark 8:1–13
Jesus heals a blind man at Bethsaida	Mark 8:22–26
Jesus heals a man born blind by spitting in his eyes	John 9:1–12
Jesus heals a boy with an unclean spirit	Matthew 17:14–20; Mark 9:14–29; Luke 9:37–43
Jesus produces the temple tax from a fish's mouth	Matthew 17:24–27
Jesus heals a blind, mute demoniac	Matthew 12:22–23; Luke 11:14–23
Jesus heals a woman who had been crippled for eighteen years	Luke 13:10–17
Jesus heals a man with dropsy on the Sabbath	Luke 14:1–6
Jesus cleanses ten lepers on the way to Jerusalem	Luke 17:11–19
Jesus raises Lazarus from the dead in Bethany	John 11:1–45
Jesus restores sight to Bartimaeus in Jericho	Matthew 20:29–34; Mark 10:46–52; Luke 18:35–43
Jesus withers the fig tree on the road from Bethany	Matthew 21:18–22; Mark 11:12–14
Jesus heals a servant's severed ear while he is being arrested	Luke 22:50–51
The second miraculous catch of fish at the Sea of Tiberias	John 21:4–11

A New Kingdom

The number one subject that Jesus taught on was something called the "kingdom of God."[11] As I write that today, it sounds very *Game of Thrones* and otherworldly. However, in that ancient time, kingdoms and empires weren't just part of the furniture, they were the room itself. In the first century in Roman-occupied Israel, a perfect storm was emerging. From one direction you had the ever-imperialistic Roman Empire pressing forth. From the other you had the thousand-year hope of the Jewish people, who were longing for their kingdom and sovereignty to be restored in their homeland. The temperature was heating up between these two worldviews. As history would seem to indicate, there could only be one winner.[12]

Enter Jesus, the itinerant teacher roaming the landscape and speaking of a so-called "kingdom of God." What was he on about? Well, as I alluded to earlier, there was some Jewish expectation that this new kingdom would be brought about through military means.[13] However, Jesus doesn't seem to conform to any of these societal expectations. The four gospel accounts in the Bible are telling the story of how Jesus becomes king of all the world.

Up until the time of Jesus, the God of the universe had almost exclusively had dealings with the Jewish people alone. But this was all about to change with Jesus. As Jesus goes about his business with the disciples, there are glimpses that the God of Israel is going to extend his reach beyond the Jewish camp. The gospel writings record travel to Gentile (non-Jewish) regions on several occasions, and Jesus performs miracles among the people there. As Jesus hangs on the cross, the gospels of Matthew (27:46) and Mark (15:34) record him citing Psalm 22 from the Old Testament, which outlines one who will undertake intense suffering but will ultimately rule over all the nations.[14]

What does this ruling look like? Well, it's not an imperialist type of rule where Jesus sits on the throne and barks instructions. He wants us to be involved in shaping a new world where the ideals of God reign and permeate throughout society as he originally intended. Folks like Caesar will still be earthly rulers, but they would be best placed to do so in the full understanding that they are not God. Someone else is ultimately in charge, and that person is Jesus.

While the greater majority of the Western world doesn't consider Jesus to be divine, they do rate Jesus as a solid moral teacher. Instructions such as love one another, be honest, work hard, manage your finances well, use your talents, are all things that the everyday person can get behind. God wants his people to thrive, and he doesn't rule in an authoritarian manner, like many of the ancient rulers of Jesus's day. He respects us as individuals and gives us the choice to follow his ways or not.

I realize it's strange to posit the idea that God/Jesus is currently reigning in this world as we speak. But if you stop for a moment and put on your historian's cap, then I don't think it's quite as ridiculous as it initially sounds. Once Jesus moved on from this world, his message spread like wildfire across the Mediterranean sphere. Generally speaking, where the message of Jesus goes, prosperity and well-being go along with it. Granted, there are some pretty horrible parts of Christian history (which are discussed in greater detail later), but on the whole, the progression of civilization to be one of flourishing would seem to follow the Christian-Judeo culture wherever it goes. I appreciate this is a subjective opinion, but others who are more qualified in this area hold a similar sentiment.

So How Does Jesus Actually Become King Then?

In short, Jesus becomes king by dying on the cross and rising from the dead three days later. How does that work? Once again, we need to have some understanding of the preceding Jewish worldview to begin to comprehend the machinations of how Jesus's death and resurrection holds significance and meaning.

1. The Temple

The Jewish temple sat prominently high on Mount Moriah, overlooking the city of Jerusalem. Its location was reflective of its significance to Jewish life. The temple was the center of national identity for the Jewish people. Further, the Jewish people believed that this was the dwelling place of the one true God. The very place where heaven and earth interconnected and overlapped with one another.[15] Its significance and the reverence the Jewish people had for it cannot be overstated.

Figure 18. Model of the Jewish Temple:
Second Temple period – Israel Museum

Credit: Dima Moroz/Shutterstock.com. Used with permission.

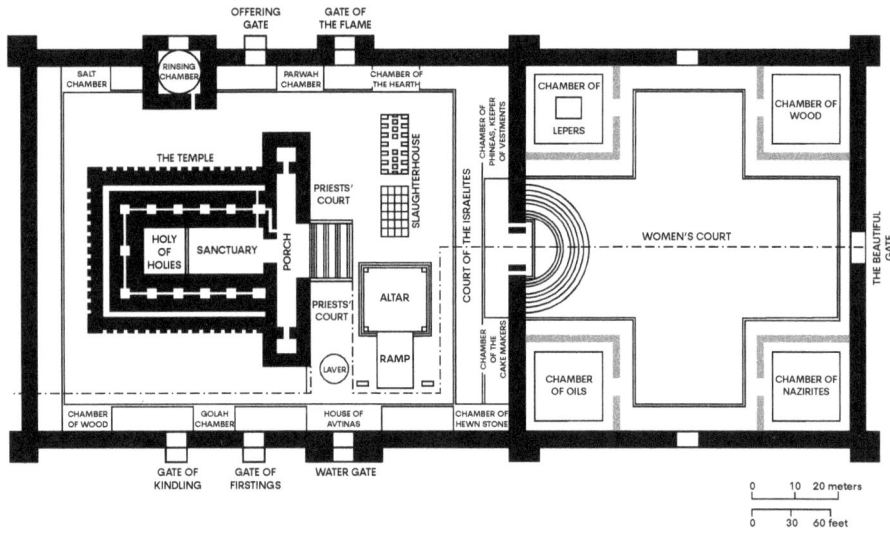

Figure 19. Layout of the Jewish Temple – Second Temple period

Credit: Achtemeier, Green, and Thompson. Redrawn with permission.

2. Sacrificial Systems

Intrinsic to the temple were the sacrificial systems, which I alluded to in phase 5 previously. Among other things, the sacrificial systems facilitated God's ability to dwell in the temple and had two fundamental purposes:

1. To appease God
2. To remove sin[16]

TO APPEASE GOD

A prominent example of a sacrifice intended to appease God is the Passover lamb. During the Hebrew period of Egyptian captivity, Moses instructed the Hebrew people to slaughter a lamb and smear the blood over the doorframes of their homes. When God passed over Egypt that night, he killed the firstborn of every household except those that had the bloodied doorframe. God killed as an act of judgment on Pharoah and the people of Egypt for how they were treating the Hebrew slaves. To have the bloodied doorframe was to appease God and his wrath. Looking ahead, the appeasement of God is also in view in various temple sacrifices that were conducted in first century Judaism.[17]

I recognize that the idea of a God who needs to be appeased is not something that we are instinctively comfortable with. I discuss this in greater detail at various points throughout the book. Suffice it to say that at this point, if we're being truly honest, we're not uncomfortable with the idea of God being angry. There are plenty of evil people that we are happy for him to exercise judgment against. The real question is whether we can trust God to fairly exercise judgment in all circumstances. I think we can trust God because of his essential nature: holiness.

Holiness is another word that we're not altogether sure how to relate to. I think the average Joe hears the word and thinks of something akin to the Benedictine monks who live a life somewhat set apart from everyday things. It's the "whiter than white" view of things, to be separated, pure, and unspoiled.

While people can relate to this mode and even appreciate the life benefits of adopting such practices on a periodic basis (think of the digital detox currently *en vogue*), I think the church's understanding and subsequent public perception of holiness is significantly incomplete. Holiness does not mean "devoid of color" and "dull" and "cut off" from the fun stuff of life. A better definition is probably "a cut above the rest," an expression used to describe something of the highest quality and utility.[18] God wants this world to work as he intended. He doesn't want you to abstain from wine, sex, and dark chocolate.

Absolutely not. He wants you to enjoy these things in the highest quality manner for which he created them.

It's when we don't enjoy these things according to his design that we enter into the unholy, subsequently risking the wrath of God. God is holy and he cannot tolerate impurity, imperfection, and corruption. I don't necessarily see a God who doles out punishment because he is angry with us for "having fun." Rather, he is angry that his creation is not functioning as he intended, that is to live a prosperous and meaningful life that is in step with his ways. Anything that gets in the way of that is best defined as sin.

TO REMOVE SIN

The animal sacrifices undertaken within the Jewish temple served to remove sin from the individual who bought the animal to be sacrificed.[19] How does that work?

The book of Leviticus in the Bible outlines in great detail how a multitude of sacrifices are to be performed in the life of the nation of Israel. When people start reading the Bible from the first book (Genesis), they tend to really enjoy it until they reach the third book (Leviticus). This listing and description of ancient practices is thoroughly disconnected from our culture at first glance, and a lot of people stop reading the Bible at this point, perhaps concluding that Christianity really is an old and outdated mode.

When I hear people express such an opinion, I have to temper my desire to call out what I would describe as a premature and immature judgment. Putting yourself in the shoes of an ancient Israelite who was looking at some of our cultural practices at first glance: How do you imagine they would view us? Would they be dismayed at our bizarre diet of social media narcissism and wholly inconsequential consumption of garbage reality TV? My point: Every culture has its weird points, so don't be simplistically judgmental.

Forgive me for my little rant as I return to the matter at hand. Six steps are involved in the sacrificial rituals. They are:

1. The offerer brings the animal to be sacrificed to the sanctuary.
2. The offerer lays his hand on the animal's head.
3. The offerer kills the animal.
4. The officiating priest carries out a blood rite (sprinkling, pouring, or applying the animal's blood).
5. The priest butchers the animal and burns the various pieces on the altar.
6. The remains are disposed of, while some cuts may be kept to be eaten.[20]

The effect of this process is consistent and repetitive in the biblical text. The priest shall make atonement on the individual's behalf for the sins that they have committed, and they shall be forgiven (Leviticus 4:35; cf. 4:20, 26, 31).

The Hebrew word *kipper* translated "make atonement" means to purge, to ransom, to expiate. There is a process here of removal, and the ultimate result is that one's sins are forgiven.[21]

How does killing an animal result in the forgiveness of one's sins? God gives us an explanation in Leviticus 17:10–11: "I will set my face against any Israelite or any foreigner residing among them who eats blood, and I will cut them off from the people. For the life of a creature is in the blood, and I have given it to you to make atonement for yourselves on the altar; it is the blood that makes atonement for one's life."

How does the shedding of blood atone for one's sin? I will echo C. S. Lewis's sentiment here from *Mere Christianity* that Christians can't actually say with any tremendous confidence how the inner workings of all this play out.[22] Ultimately, what is clear to me is that the Bible makes it plain that the shedding of blood was a God-given institution with a clear intention, that being to atone for one's life.

With the Framework Set, Enter Jesus

The iconic Da Vinci painting of the Last Supper depicts Jesus's final meal with his disciples. At this occasion, Jesus explicitly outlines the purpose of his impending death: to create a new covenant through the shedding of his blood for the forgiveness of sins (Matthew 26:28).[23] Additionally, the fact that such a declaration was carried out at the commemoration of the Passover is important. Jesus was probably identifying himself as the ultimate Passover sacrifice,[24] thus displaying that his death diverts the wrath of God that was due to fall upon us.

Jesus then gets crucified. The gospel accounts, in varying detail, put forth that an earthquake and a three-hour darkening of the sun took place while Jesus was still hanging on the cross (Matthew 27:45–54; Mark 15:33; Luke 23:44). Given the claims of such major natural phenomena, it would seem prudent to explore whether there is any other evidence to support these events' legitimacy. I've summarized the available evidence in the table below, which I consider to be inconclusive, yet interesting:

Table 9: Evidence of Sun Darkening

Author	Proposed Account
Thallus – A Greek chronographer who published work in three books covering the period of the Assyrian King Belus to at least the death of Christ.[25]	Georgius Syncellus cites Sextus Julius Africanus, who in turn cites Thallus, who refers to the darkness that occurred at the death of Jesus. Thallus explains away the darkness as a natural phenomenon; Africanus objects and asserts that the darkness was a miracle. Either way, and assuming such citations are true, it was agreed that a darkness (whatever the cause) took place. All this means that Thallus may be the earliest non-Christian of whom we have record potentially referring to the gospel account.[26]
Phlegon – A Greek author who wrote a work covering all of the Olympiads from the first to AD 140.[27]	The Christian writers Jerome and Origen cite Phlegon as confirming the darkness and earthquakes taking place during the period of Jesus's crucifixion.[28]

It has been argued that if these supposed events really did occur, then they would have been recorded in other works by Seneca, Pliny, or Josephus.[29] Yes, one could make that argument. Thinking it through, however, one could make the counterargument that for Roman historians to acknowledge and publicize such events, which ultimately represented a significant defeat for the Roman Empire, would have been a seriously career-limiting move—that was in all likelihood the reason for such an omission.

The four gospel accounts are consistent in their accounting that Jesus died on the cross and his body was placed in a tomb by a wealthy follower of Jesus called Joseph of Arimathea (Matthew 27:50-61; Mark 15:37-47; Luke 23:46-53; John 19:30-42). They also consistently record Jesus coming back to life on the third day and appearing to his disciples (Matthew 28:1-20; Mark 16:1-14; Luke 24:1-43; John 20:1-20). Jesus then remained for another forty days, spending time with his disciples (Acts 1:3) and other people, in excess of five hundred according to the apostle Paul in 1 Corinthians 15:6, until he ascended to heaven (Luke 24:51; Acts 1:9).

I have always found the forty-day post-resurrection period somewhat peculiar in that the Roman authorities seemingly made no effort to rearrest Jesus. I've often thought that the lack of such an attestation takes credibility away from the resurrection accounts. Surely the Romans would want to interrogate Jesus at the very least? That said, perhaps such an interrogation did actually take place but we have no record of it.

The perceived lack of Roman interest is probably reasonable to expect given the circumstances. If they had crucified the Son of God, then out of self-preservation the last place they would want to be was in his immediate presence. The additional proposition of having another crucifixion attempt at Jesus would be even more unattractive to them. I still find it peculiar that we don't have any record of Jesus's interaction with the authorities, but that is the picture that we have and we must leave it be.

No doubt, the disciples would have been pretty bewildered with all the above goings on. Roaming across the countryside, watching Jesus perform miracles, upsetting the religious leaders, seeing their leader be crucified, only to then have him come back to life. Your head would be spinning. During this forty-day period, they must have been clarifying a few things with Jesus.

Why did Jesus die on the cross and rise again? Well, it's multifaceted. There has been so much written on the subject for centuries, but I think there are three major pillars from which all other commentary flows:

1. Jesus Died for Our Sins

The pre-existence of the temple's sacrificial system, Jesus's own understanding of the purpose of his impending death, and the subsequent interpretation of Jesus's death by the other New Testament writers all lead to the conclusion that Jesus died for our sins.[30] Jesus's disciple Peter wrote, "For Christ also suffered once for sins, the righteous for the unrighteous, to bring you to God. He was put to death in the body but made alive in the Spirit" (1 Peter 3:18).

Another disciple, John, wrote, "But if we walk in the light, as he is in the light, we have fellowship with one another, and the blood of Jesus, his Son, purifies us from all sin" (1 John 1:7).

And in Revelation, John wrote, "And from Jesus Christ, who is the faithful witness, the firstborn from the dead, and the ruler of the kings of the earth. To him who loves us and has freed us from our sins by his blood" (Revelation 1:5).

The apostle and close contact of the disciples, Paul, wrote, "For what I received I passed on to you as of first importance: that Christ died for our sins according to the Scriptures" (1 Corinthians 15:3).

And the author of Hebrews wrote:

> Otherwise Christ would have had to suffer many times since the creation of the world. But he has appeared once for all at the culmination of the ages to do away with sin by the sacrifice of himself. Just as people are destined to die once, and after that to face judgment, so Christ was sacrificed once to take away the sins of many; and he will appear a second time, not to bear sin, but to bring salvation to those who are waiting for him. (Hebrews 9:26–28)

Note that two of the above texts declare that Christ died once and for all. Whereas the sacrifices in the temple system need to be repeated, Jesus's sacrifice did not. A powerful image and event that undergirds this is the tearing of the temple veil at the point of Jesus's death.

If you take a look at the temple diagram in Figure 19 on page 90, you will see a section called the Holy of Holies. This was the place where the true living God dwelt in Judaism. It was separated from the outer sanctuary by a veil. No one was permitted to penetrate the veil except the high priest, who did so once a year on the Day of Atonement.[31] Three of the gospel accounts record that the veil of the temple was torn in two from top to bottom at the point of Jesus's death on the cross (Matthew 27:51; Mark 15:38; Luke 23:45).

The torn veil indicates that God was making the institution of the temple and its complex system of sacrifices and worship practices redundant.[32] God was no longer to dwell in a room isolated from his people by a veil. He was instituting something new. Something that subsequent New Testament writers and believers in Jesus would have to flesh out in the midst of all that had gone before them in Judaism.

2. Jesus Has Established a New World Order and Become King

As I mentioned earlier in this chapter, the four gospel accounts tell the story of how Jesus became king over all creation. This was finalized with his death on the cross and resurrection. Jesus performed miracles and loved those who weren't deemed worthy by the earthly rulers and powers. He never picked up a sword or conspired to hurt people, whether through physical violence or political means. He dialogued with people, engaged with their struggles, and sought to get to the heart of the matter of life's biggest questions (which were regularly posed to him). He never sought praise, position, or recognition; rather, he sought to divert accolades and let his good deeds be just that: good deeds worthy in their own right. He served others when he should have been served. Despite all this, the earthly powers—both religious leaders and political custodians—would not yield to his tidal wave of love and miracles.

Ultimately, what seemingly scared them was having to yield and relinquish their own power and trust. They wanted to be in charge. They embarked on the one ultimate power move: taking his life. Jesus willingly, not showing a shred of obstruction, submitted to this death. I would love to say that Jesus threw out the taunt "Do your best" to his ignorant accusers, but Jesus is so much better than my angry self. He was the ultimate example of humility, calm, and service right to the very end. Even hanging naked on the cross, experiencing the greatest human pain and shame, he still found the energy to utter the words, "Father, forgive them, for they do not know what they are doing" (Luke 23:34).

Jesus, then, did the ultimate power move in response: He rose from the dead. Death couldn't contain him, and with that, the earthly rulers' game was up. Jesus is fully in charge, and this is probably evidenced by the conspicuous absence of his executioners and accusers in the post-resurrection period. Did Jesus do a spike in the end zone to signify his triumphant touchdown? There's no indication of that, just a loving and accepting embrace of his disciples who abandoned and shunned any known association with him. His disciples would ultimately follow in his example, all going to their deaths in martyrdom.

3. Jesus's Death and Resurrection Kickstarts a Movement Where You Play a Part

The previous two points aren't just dormant theological concepts sitting in the history books. They are intended to be active and disruptive mechanisms by which the one true creator God transforms this world into the design he intended. Jesus has died for our sins and modeled the ideals of kingship for us so that we can live a life that God intends for us as individuals and as a community. It's a baffling concept to try and understand, let alone communicate. The idea that God is interested in me and requires things of me to cultivate this world is frankly laughable. Why would the all-powerful creator God need me? The truth is, he doesn't need me, but he wants me. Ever since the dawn of time, God has wanted humankind to be in a symbiotic relationship with him. As I said earlier in this book, God doesn't impose himself on us. Rather, he has given us the freedom to choose his ways or not. I believe that

CHAPTER 6: WHAT DO THE MIRACLES MEAN?

God is speaking to you right now through my words. I feel the weight of that statement; one wouldn't want to misquote God through their own fallible nature. But it seems that God is choosing me as his spokesperson, and I hope I get this right. In essence, I think God is saying this:

> *Look, you know that stuff inside of you, the stuff that you carry around in your mind and heart but don't dare share with anyone, lest it reveal your weakness, humanity, and inadequacy. Well, I've dealt with that on the cross. It can't separate you from me anymore, nor can it rule your life. I have dealt with it. But you have to yield it to me. Not only do you have to yield your insecurities, weaknesses, and faults, but you have to yield your very own life. I want all of you, and I have plans for you. Choose my ways and you choose life. My kingship is different from the ways of the world. I'll be honest with you; some days will be really hard. You'll be tempted to go your own way. But if you stay with me, I promise you'll be okay.*

I hope that in this chapter I've done justice to the most significant life ever lived on planet earth. Jesus's death and resurrection was not a party trick. It has complexity, sophistication, and multiple world-changing elements that we, as Christians, continue to reflect upon to this day.

In order for the cross to have a meaningful impact on you, you need to first recognize the concept of sin, both in the world around you and in yourself. Many people don't consider themselves sinful. It won't come as a surprise, then, that the cross is just a historical happening to them, carrying no significance and relevance. If sin doesn't exist, then such a view is right and fair, rendering the cross somewhat aimless. It's only prudent that we consider the concept of sin in the next chapter.

CHAPTER 7

DOES OBJECTIVE MORALITY EXIST?

C. S. Lewis wrote, "These, then, are the two points I wanted to make. First, that human beings, all over the earth, have this curious idea that they ought to behave in a certain way, and cannot really get rid of it. Secondly, that they do not in fact behave in that way. They know the Law of Nature and they break it."[1]

In the previous chapter, I introduced the concept of sin and explained how Jesus's existence addresses this concept. To believe in something called "sin" is to accept that an objective morality exists—something like what C. S. Lewis alluded to above.

What Is Objective Morality?

I want to use the definition of objective morality that William Lane Craig put forward:

> In any given situation that you might find yourself, there is something that is really right and really wrong independently of human opinion, but clearly that might vary with the circumstances. In some cases it would be morally permissible to kill, but in other cases it would be morally impermissible to kill. So, what I'm talking about is objective right and wrong but not necessarily absolutes that take no cognizance of the circumstances in which a person finds their self.[2]

When I have discussions regarding worldview and religion, I nearly always find consensus with those participating that objective morality exists.

In fact, I would argue that objective morality is the number one argument the new-atheist movement uses to discredit religion. They say that religion causes more harm than good and that it doesn't live up to basic universal moral standards.

If it can be agreed that objective morality exists, then an inquiring mind will search for an explanation pertaining to its origins.

Where Does Objective Morality Come From?

1. Objective Morality Has a Darwinian Origin

Richard Dawkins argues that our objective morality is derived from our Darwinian roots. He puts forward that we have four good Darwinian reasons for individuals to be altruistic, generous, or "moral" toward each other. To summarize, Dawkins suggests that we are biologically wired to:

1. Look after our own kin because we are genetically disposed to do so
2. Show generosity to others because we want that generosity to be reciprocated
3. Foster a good reputation to facilitate reciprocity
4. Be conspicuously generous to greater emphasize one's reputation and enable reciprocity

While these principles summarize seemingly "selfish" behaviors, Dawkins does address the dilemma of how to explain unselfish altruistic behavior that we see in the everyday world. He explains that the above Darwinian principles would best be described as "rules of thumb." In his book *The God Delusion*, he writes:

> Rules of thumb, by their nature, sometimes misfire. In a bird's brain, the rule "Look after small squawking things in your nest, and drop food into their red gapes" typically has the effect of preserving the genes that built the rule, because the squawking, gaping objects in an adult bird's nest are normally its own offspring. The rule misfires if another baby bird somehow gets into the nest, a circumstance that is positively engineered by cuckoos. Could it be that our Good Samaritan urges

are misfirings, analogous to the misfiring of a reed warbler's parental instincts when it works itself to the bone for a young cuckoo? An even closer analogy is the human urge to adopt a child. I must rush to add that "misfiring" is intended only in a strictly Darwinian sense. It carries no suggestion of the pejorative.[3]

At first hearing, Dawkins's view sounds somewhat degrading of generous acts, and he rightly senses this. He goes on to add that these misfirings are "Darwinian mistakes: blessed, precious mistakes. Do not, for one moment, think of such Darwinizing as demeaning or reductive of the noble emotions of compassion and generosity."[4]

In part, I find Dawkins's view somewhat logical. I am not an evolutionary biologist, and there is nothing in me that instinctively disagrees with his four Darwinian principles that perhaps influence those aforementioned human behaviors. However, I feel rather unfulfilled by his accounting for altruistic behavior as a hypothesized "misfiring." As I just quoted, Dawkins describes these misfirings as being:

- Blessed
- Precious
- Noble

Dawkins's language certainly implies that such altruistic acts have deep intrinsic value and worth. Yet, he doesn't put forward an origin for this supposed value.

In addition, Dawkins gapingly doesn't discuss non-altruistic behavior in his chapter on morality. In chapter 2 of the same book, he says, "The God of the Old Testament is arguably the most unpleasant character in all fiction: jealous and proud of it; a petty, unjust, unforgiving control-freak; a vindictive, bloodthirsty ethnic cleanser; a misogynistic, homophobic, racist, infanticidal, genocidal, filicidal, pestilential, megalomaniacal, sadomasochistic, capriciously malevolent bully."[5]

Dawkins has not explained how he has ascertained his moral framework to judge God or any other supposedly "wrong" behavior or trait. To provide a Darwinian framework to explain how good comes about is one thing, but to explain how good and bad exist in the first instance is another matter entirely.

In summary, I think Dawkins's accounting for an objective morality generates more questions than answers.

2. Objective Morality Exists and Is Necessary for the Proliferation of Human Life

When I lived in London, I attended periodic events at the London Atheist Activist Group. I would often ask the members how they explained the existence of an objective morality, and the most common answer was that a morality system existed to ensure the proliferation of human life.

It's an interesting response for which I always asked the follow up question, "How is the proliferation of human life necessary or important?" One common response was that the proliferation of human life isn't necessary, it's just good practice and better for the world. As you can see, this is circular reasoning; my original question asked by what means we account for good and evil (morality), and the answer is that life is inherently good. We're back at the start again.

Another response (albeit rarer at the group) was that life was important and meaningful and thus its proliferation should be pursued. Personally, I agree with this answer and it marries well with a Christian worldview; however, it doesn't marry so well with an atheistic worldview, which predominantly espouses that there is no inherent meaning to life.

As such, I somewhat agree with the proliferation argument; however, I think it only really works when viewed through a theistic lens.

3. Objective Morality Just Exists

An explanation, and yet not an explanation, for the existence of objective morality is that it just exists. We can't explain it or make sense of it, but there seems to be moral law that the majority of human beings can agree with on a regular basis.

I have often found in the midst of debate that atheists and agnostics alike are right on the cusp of making such an assertion but stop themselves at the last minute. I sense they stop because they know that to make such an assertion is akin to the Christian saying that "God just exists," which is never digested well by atheists (and nor should it be for that matter).

In summary, I don't have a philosophical objection to the statement that objective morality just exists. Yes, it could just exist, but I remain open to an alternative explanation of its origins. I find the "it just exists" argument to be wholly insubstantial.

4. God Is the Maker and Giver of an Objective Morality

At first hearing, some might say that to attribute objective morality to a supreme being is a "god of the gaps" scenario, meaning we attribute the origin of objective morality to God because we have no better way of accounting for its existence otherwise.

For me personally as a Christian, I do this in part. However, for the other part, I think that a philosophical rationale can be presented to demonstrate that attributing the existence of morality to God is not entirely a "god of the gaps" leap. For instance, for an objective moral law to exist, then it seems reasonable that an ultimate judge or enforcer needs to exist as well.

Can you think of a country where there is no police, and societal order reigns in abundance? I have traveled to countries where there is legal enforcement, and I have traveled to those where there is little. It is clear to me which countries I prefer.

It's not simply that these better countries have laws. They have laws with enforcement. This begs the question: Can a law truly exist without enforcement?

If we are so sure of objective morality, can we be sure it can exist without enforcement or oversight? My life experience suggests to me that a law is only a law if there is an overarching judgment methodology and framework that is evaluative and authoritative. If objective moral law exists, what is the judgment framework that makes it substantive and binding? I think that the idea of God is the only reasonable rationale for the judgment framework that would need to exist to sustain objective morality.

In summary, I want to make it very clear that I am not suggesting that the existence of an objective morality proves that God exists. Rather, I think that God is the best and most plausible explanation for the existence of an objective morality out of all the theories that have been discussed in this chapter. Objective morality doesn't prove God's existence, but it should add to the weight of evidence that he exists.

Where to Go from Here?

It would seem logical that if you believe in the possibility of an objective morality coming from God or something else, then you will need to do some further digging to see whether God has had anything salient to say on the matter through the annals of history. Further, you would want to gain an understanding of the character of God to see whether he, in fact, lives up to his so-called objective morality. In the upcoming chapters, we will further investigate whether the God of Christianity is indeed a moral one.

CHAPTER 8

IS GOD A GENOCIDAL MANIAC?

Steven Pinker states, "The scriptures present a God who delights in genocide, rape, slavery, and the execution of nonconformists."[1]

This is decisive language from one of the world's most notable atheists. Does the assessment match the alleged crime? In this chapter we will analyze the more specific question of whether the Christian God is a genocidal maniac.

Is God a Bloodthirsty Ethnic Cleanser?

A commonly opinion held by many non-Christians and some Christians is that the God depicted in the Old Testament is all about war. The New Testament is viewed as pleasant, loving, and fluffy—resembling an episode of *Happy Days* (crucifixion exempted). However, the Old Testament is more like *Game of Thrones* and then some. Is this true?

There are some stories in the Old Testament that certainly make for difficult reading. One of them I have already referred to in chapter 3, namely the battle for Jericho.

To reiterate, the story goes as follows:

1. God instructs the Israelites to totally destroy the people of Jericho (Deuteronomy 7:2).
2. Joshua (Israel's leader) sends two spies to Jericho where they are helped by the prostitute Rahab. In return, the spies guarantee the safety of Rahab and her family during the subsequent invasion (Joshua 2).

3. Joshua and the army of Israel march around the city of Jericho for seven days (Joshua 6:14–15).
4. On the seventh day of marching, the trumpets sound and the army of Israel shouts; the walls of Jericho collapse, allowing the invasion of the Israelites (Joshua 6:20).
5. The Israelite army destroys every living thing in the city, including men, women, children, and livestock (Joshua 6:21).
6. Rahab and her family are spared from the bloodshed per the earlier guarantee (Joshua 6:22-23).

Genocide is defined in the *Oxford English Dictionary* as "the deliberate killing of a large group of people, especially those of a particular nation or ethnic group."[2]

According to this definition, we could conclude that the God of the Old Testament has indeed caused genocide. If Christianity claims that God's character is one of love, how does it account for genocide?

First, we need to ask why God gave such an instruction to the people of Israel in this instance. Biblical narratives in the books of Deuteronomy and Leviticus outline that Jericho was a very immoral society that practiced incest and child sacrifice.[3] When the two spies met with Rahab prior to the invasion, she said:

> I know that the Lord has given you this land and that a great fear of you has fallen on us, so that all who live in this country are melting in fear because of you. We have heard how the Lord dried up the water of the Red Sea for you when you came out of Egypt, and what you did to Sihon and Og, the two kings of the Amorites east of the Jordan, whom you completely destroyed. When we heard of it, our hearts melted in fear and everyone's courage failed because of you, for the Lord your God is God in heaven above and on the earth below. (Joshua 2:9-11)

Given that Rahab knew about the acts of the Israelites, it is reasonable to deduce that the other residents of Jericho had similar knowledge. Thus, it could be argued that these other residents had adequate and sufficient opportunity to surrender to the Israelites as Rahab effectively did. However, no such surrender is indicated to have taken place apart from Rahab and her family.

Deuteronomy 9:4–6 says:

> After the Lord your God has driven them out before you, do not say to yourself, "The Lord has brought me here to take possession of this land because of my righteousness." No, it is on account of the wickedness of these nations that the Lord is going to drive them out before you. It is not because of your righteousness or your integrity that you are going in to take possession of their land; but on account of the wickedness of these nations, the Lord your God will drive them out before you, to accomplish what he swore to your fathers, to Abraham, Isaac and Jacob. Understand, then, that it is not because of your righteousness that the Lord your God is giving you this good land to possess, for you are a stiff-necked people.

Just prior to the invasion of Jericho, Israel's military leader, Joshua, has a vision of an angelic figure called "the commander of the LORD's army." Joshua asks, "Are you for us or for them?" The figure replies, "Neither" (Joshua 5:13–15).

We can see from the biblical account that God was certainly not delighting or celebrating in what he commanded the armies of Israel to do. The invasion and destruction of Jericho is portrayed by the Bible as an act of God's judgment on the morally corrupt culture of Canaan. It is a disturbing story, and I can certainly perceive a sense that God perhaps really didn't want it to be this way. Something of a lamenting spirit certainly lingers in the atmosphere of all this. It certainly doesn't match Richard Dawkins's description in the previous chapter that God is capricious, unjust, and petty.

The rest of the book of Joshua doesn't make for easier reading. Battle after battle, sanctioned by God, leaves anyone with a sense of sadness and internal conflict. On one hand, I recognize the idea that God is bringing judgment and wrath to an evil culture, and I can somewhat understand that. On the other hand, I struggle with the concept that relatively innocent people would most probably have been caught up in these atrocities. These are difficult emotions to reconcile. Miroslav Volf writes:

> I used to think that wrath was unworthy of God. Isn't God love? Shouldn't divine love be beyond wrath? God is love, and God loves every person and every creature. That's exactly why God is wrathful against some of them. My last resistance to the idea of God's wrath was a casualty of the war in the former Yugoslavia, the region from which I come. According to some estimates, 200,000 people were killed and over 3 million were displaced. My villages and cities were destroyed, my people shelled day in day out, some of them brutalized beyond imagination and I could not imagine God not being angry. Or think of Rwanda in the last decade of the last century, where 800,000 people were hacked to death in one hundred days! How did God react to the carnage? By doting on the perpetrators' basic goodness? Wasn't God fiercely angry with them? Though I used to complain about the indecency of the idea of God's wrath, I came to think that I would have to rebel against a God who wasn't wrathful at the sight of the world's evil. God isn't wrathful in spite of love. God is wrathful because God is love.[4]

So where to from here? Well, in a similar vein to our discussion in chapter 2 on suffering, we could conclude that God is a genocidal maniac, fundamentally immoral, and not worthy of our attention and submission. On the other hand, one could choose to give God the benefit of the doubt here, to see that perhaps our humanity is not capable of judging God in this respect and that we're best placed to be cautious rather than dismissive.

Perhaps God could see a bigger picture here and that the right thing was to exercise violence in these instances? It's still an incredibly hard thing to contemplate; however, I think being open to this possibility is the more prudent approach and that one should not dismiss God altogether.

CHAPTER 9

IS GOD A PROMOTER OF SLAVERY?

The Old Testament of the Bible says:

> Your male and female slaves are to come from the nations around you; from them you may buy slaves. You may also buy some of the temporary residents living among you and members of their clans born in your country, and they will become your property. You can bequeath them to your children as inherited property and can make them slaves for life, but you must not rule over your fellow Israelites ruthlessly. (Leviticus 25:44–46)

> Anyone who beats their male or female slave with a rod must be punished if the slave dies as a direct result, but they are not to be punished if the slave recovers after a day or two, since the slave is their property. (Exodus 21:20–21)

The New Testament of the Bible says:

> Slaves, obey your earthly masters with respect and fear, and with sincerity of heart, just as you would obey Christ. Obey them not only to win their favor when their eye is on you, but as slaves of Christ, doing the will of God from your heart. Serve wholeheartedly, as if you were serving the Lord, not people, because you know that the Lord will reward each one for whatever good they do, whether they are slave or free. (Ephesians 6:5–8)

The argument that the Bible supports slavery goes something like this:

1. Bible translations talk of slaves.
2. In the Old Testament, no objection is made to slavery.
3. In the New Testament, Christians are not commanded to free their slaves and slaves are told to submit.
4. Therefore, biblical texts approve of slavery.
5. We know that slavery is wrong.
6. Therefore, biblical texts approve of something that is wrong.[1]

When we see the word "slavery," the very worst of humanity comes into our minds. No good can surely come from the word, and just the sheer presence of it in the Bible causes us to shudder and despair. So, what is a supposedly loving God doing by seemingly endorsing such a barbaric practice?

Well, let's take a look at each of the premises in the argument just put forth.

1. Bible Translations Talk of Slaves

You may remember from my previous chapter that the Old Testament of the Bible was originally written in Hebrew and subsequently translated in multiple time periods and languages. Well, the original word for "slave" is the Hebrew word *ebed*.

While our modern English language is very large, ancient Hebrew is comprised of far fewer words. As such, one individual Hebrew word is often translated into multiple English words depending on what the scholarship decides is the best translation. As you can imagine, this is often a very challenging task, and we should always remember this when we endeavor to interpret the Bible.

Ebed is translated into either "slave" or "servant" within the Old Testament. These English words can mean very different things.[2]

There is a debate at present as to whether *ebed* should be translated "servant" or "slave." For a more detailed analysis of this current debate, please see Peter Williams's lecture, "Does the Bible Support Slavery?," which is cited in footnote 1 of this chapter. However, if it were to be translated "servant," then it could be argued that the first and second premise of the aforementioned argument evaporates.

To adopt a more skeptical disposition, however, let's proceed with our analysis on the assumption that *ebed* is rightly translated "slave" in these instances.

Now, let's move onto the second premise.

2. In the Old Testament, No Objection Is Made to Slavery

Assuming the above translation of *ebed* is correct, then we can confidently say that the Old Testament makes no objection to one having slaves. However, if I don't raise an objection to something, does that automatically equal advocacy of that very thing?

If I'm at a dinner party and the person next to me voices that they think that the Christian religion is a fraud, then I may or may not voice an alternative view to that person. I will consider a wide variety of factors including:

1. The relative importance of the issue
2. The suitability of the environment to have a conversation of that nature
3. Whether the person is open to hearing a different viewpoint

I imagine there have been many occasions where you and I have decided not to voice an alternate position after considering these very factors. However, that doesn't mean we are in support of the aforementioned view.

Absence of objection doesn't automatically equal advocacy of a particular view.

However, I can appreciate that the Old Testament references to slavery are still troubling, and it would be preferable to get a greater sense of what is going on with these texts. With that in mind, I will now talk about these passages further.

The Texts

Exodus 21:20–21 is particularly disturbing, as it seems to advocate for the beating of slaves, which does present us with an ugly reminder of

New World slavery. Let us read the verse again: "Anyone who beats their male or female slave with a rod must be punished if the slave dies as a direct result, but they are not to be punished if the slave recovers after a day or two, since the slave is their property" (Exodus 21:20–21).

At a first reading, we could interpret this verse as effectively saying that the slave owner can do what they like with their slave because, after all, the slave is "their property."

However, let's read the expanded passage, which provides a more detailed context:

> If people quarrel and one person hits another with a stone or with their fist and the victim does not die but is confined to bed, the one who struck the blow will not be held liable if the other can get up and walk around outside with a staff; however, the guilty party must pay the injured person for any loss of time and see that the victim is completely healed.
>
> Anyone who beats their male or female slave with a rod must be punished if the slave dies as a direct result, but they are not to be punished if the slave recovers after a day or two, since the slave is their property. (Exodus 21:18–21)
>
> [Four verses later.] An owner who hits a male or female slave in the eye and destroys it must let the slave go free to compensate for the eye. And an owner who knocks out the tooth of a male or female slave must let the slave go free to compensate for the tooth. (Exodus 21:26–27)

These additional verses make it clear that the Bible cannot be instructing slave owners to do whatever they like with their slaves. If this was the case, then why would a slave owner have to let their slave go for knocking the slave's tooth out?

We need to understand that this passage is outlining case law. Case law does not approve of the situations for which it is legislating. For instance, in a modern Western society, we have laws that punish people for murder. It would be nonsensical to say that our society permits murder simply because it legislates punishment for its occurrence. Similarly, this passage in Exodus is not sanctioning beating a slave or even slavery simply for stating what is to happen under circumstances involving a slave and their master.[3]

However, regardless of whether the Bible advocates for good or bad treatment of slaves, we are still not comfortable with the idea that someone can "own" another person. After all, Exodus 21:21 says, "since the slave is their *property*" (emphasis added).

When we hear the word "slavery," most of us will immediately think of the slavery that was practiced from the sixteenth century onward, most notably in North America. To equate that type of slavery with the slavery that is referenced in the biblical passages above is premature. Scholars of this ancient region are quick to point out that nowhere do we see the kind of mass exploitation that we find in the sixteenth century and onward.[4]

While it's mildly comforting that slavery in the Old Testament and the ancient Near East was probably nowhere near as bad as the atrocities seen in New World slavery, this hardly puts the issue to bed. Surely a loving God wouldn't permit *any* form of slavery to take place, no matter how much better it was than other forms.

At this point, I think it is important that we try to insert ourselves into the economic framework that a person living in the Old Testament period would experience. As I write this chapter, our world is currently trying to negotiate the coronavirus pandemic with mixed success. World governments have responded quickly with stimulus packages and economic relief to their citizens. A relief package can be announced one week, and those funds are released to businesses and individuals the following week, seemingly at the touch of a button.

The biblical landscape was very different economically. There was no electronic financial system, banks, fluid labor markets, social security, nationalized healthcare, or sophisticated justice system in place. When a person or family experienced economic hardship, they didn't join a social security line. They couldn't rely on a government to create debt at the drop of a hat to prop up its citizens. The sheer reality is that they probably knocked on a door and offered themselves as slaves or servants for a period in exchange for food and shelter. Slavery wasn't an optional extra in this economic landscape. It was a fixture of the economic framework.

At this point, we need to remind ourselves what the Bible is and what it isn't. The Bible isn't an IKEA instruction manual that tells you exactly and precisely what you need to do in every single life situation. As you and I know, our world is tremendously complicated at times, and the Bible throws itself into this landscape to help us navigate life's challenges.

The Bible is sometimes *descriptive and not prescriptive*. Did the people of Israel improperly use slavery to their own advantage? Possibly. Does the Old Testament endorse this practice? No, it does not. It is describing how Israel managed slavery, not whether it was the right thing to do in the first instance.

With that said, let us now turn our attention to the third premise of the argument.

3. In the New Testament, Christians Are Not Commanded to Free Their Slaves and Slaves Are Told to Submit

At first reading, it would seem that the New Testament is stronger in its support of slavery than the Old Testament by explicitly supporting it rather than just recognizing the institution and regulating it as the Old Testament does. The apostle Paul gives this explicit instruction: "Slaves, obey your earthly masters with respect and fear" (Ephesians 6:5).

What is going on here?

There are a couple of different directions that one could take. One could conclude that Paul was *pro-slavery*. He had several clear opportunities to denounce the practice and start the necessary revolution; however, there is no evidence that any of this took place.

Another could conclude that Paul was *ambivalent to the institution of slavery*. The Roman slavery expert Ulrike Roth outlines that Christian slaves in the

Greco-Roman world were somewhat independent from their masters economically,[5] in vast contrast to the type of New World slavery that we envision today. These slaves had access to their master's funds and were able to operate businesses on their own—both for their own individual benefit and for their master's benefit. Some were even able to amass considerable fortunes.[6]

Paul wrote the letter of Philemon to the slave owner Philemon regarding an apparent conflict between this master and his slave, Onesimus. Paul controversially recommends that Onesimus returns to his master Philemon (v. 12). Roth describes Onesimus's slave status in the following terms:

> A slave with access to the master's funds, or trusted with money (and potentially financial business), who appears learned and skilled enough to be considered an active contributor to missionary activity, and whose labor duties involve freedom of movement, including independent travelling, recalls more readily the type of slave made famous by Cicero in his *a manu* Tiro, or Gamliel's Tabi, than the slave set to work in the mines who was caricatured by Plautus in the second century BCE as "kept in chains" by his underground workplace.

Roth goes on to say:

> Obviously, it is impossible to prove that Onesimus, or any other servile Christian, including the abovementioned "saints" from "the household of Caesar" (which later texts viewed as a source of converts), indeed benefitted from the enjoyment of their own funds, or that they could have used such funds at their own discretion, but their cultic activity independent of their owners—in one case, the Roman emperor—is remarkable and suggestive.[7]

Perhaps given the relative well-being of these "slaves," Paul didn't consider it necessary to address the institution directly. After all, he was primarily interested in promoting the newly established Christian faith far and wide, not addressing all of life's issues in one go.

A third theory is that Paul *did care about the institution of slavery deeply and if he had his perfect way it would have been abolished there and then, but he didn't address the issue because it wasn't practical or realistic to do so.* Throughout Paul's letters in the New Testament, he insists on the equality of slaves among all people in the church.[8] In 1 Corinthians 12:13, he says, "For we were all baptized by one Spirit so as to form one body—whether Jews or Gentiles, slave or free—and we were all given the one Spirit to drink." Similarly in Colossians 3:11, he writes, "Here there is no Gentile or Jew, circumcised or uncircumcised, barbarian, Scythian, slave or free, but Christ is all, and is in all." And in Galatians 3:28, he says, "There is neither Jew nor Gentile, neither slave nor free, nor is there male and female, for you are all one in Christ Jesus."

If Paul is keen on the equality of slaves, why doesn't he denounce the practice?

According to the Roman law of *Lex Fufia Caninia*, established in 2 BC, there were limits to the emancipation of slaves. Under this law, a slave owner could release:

- Two slaves if they held three
- Half of their slaves if they held four to ten slaves
- A third of their slaves if they held eleven to thirty slaves

If all of one's slaves were released, or if any slaves rebelled, then they would have most likely been executed by Roman crucifixion—hardly an ideal outcome.

Another restriction was that slaves under the age of thirty who were freed were never able to become Roman citizens.[9]

All in all, it seems reasonable to see that Paul and other Christian leaders had to work within strict societal parameters and legal systems that made it difficult to tackle the issue of embedded slavery head on. Paul's concern was primarily with the expansion of the Christian church, and he was probably trying to be careful to not create unnecessary fires that would have significantly hampered his mission.

I once heard a story about a young boy who was being bullied on a school bus. There were several boys who were ganging up on this one kid, shouting obscenity after obscenity at him. Several rows behind the bullied boy sat another young student who was one of the more popular and physically prominent boys. Becoming aggrieved and angry with the situation, this boy stood up, walked toward the boy being teased, and sat down next to him. He never said a word, and the teasing stopped. This boy didn't have to use physical violence or any other form of intimidation. He sent a very clear and powerful message to those other boys that day: This boy being teased was an equal among them all, and he was to be treated as such.

Likewise, we see in the New Testament that Jesus and Paul enter into the very status of slavery themselves. During his Last Supper with his disciples, Jesus undertook the role of foot-washer, which was traditionally performed by slaves. He washed each disciple's feet (to their horror). Paul frequently referred to himself as a slave of Christ in his writings.[10] All of this, to me, is the equivalent of sitting next to the kid on the bus. The Son of God and the most senior leader of the early Christian church placing themselves within the very institution of slavery powerfully removes the shame of being a slave, replacing it with honor, dignity, and belonging.

I think that the totality of evidence points to a greater support of this third theory that Paul opposed slavery but permitted its existence in the pursuit of a greater good.

Conclusion

In conclusion, there seem to be two main options here in dealing with the question of slavery in the Bible. One can view the Bible as supporting slavery and, therefore, as immoral and not worthy of modern-day consideration and analysis. The alternative view is that the Bible worked within the confines of society and was descriptive rather than prescriptive in certain instances.

In three hundred years, people may be bewildered that individuals like you and I were still driving cars and taking cheap flights around the globe while knowing that it was probably killing the planet and subsequent future generations. If our carbon catastrophe is true, then is it also true that the greatest advocates of a response to climate change are being openly hypocritical in driving their cars and charging their phones every day? In some ways yes, and in some ways no. To enact change within the key pillars of our economic framework is very difficult, and these changes don't happen overnight, as in the case of slavery.[11] Perhaps in light of this, we should be careful not to be overly judgmental of the Bible.

CHAPTER 10

IS GOD A MISOGYNIST?

In short, I think God is not a misogynist. However, I can empathize with people who may see it differently given the church's track record and humankind's broader performance of how we have treated and viewed women through the ages.

Before we get into the details here, I want us to revisit a principle that I raised in the last chapter regarding description versus prescription. The Bible describes many historical events, but we must be careful not to equate description with endorsement. This principle will help us see what the Bible really says rather than assume we understand what it is saying.

Many argue that the Bible portrays a God who is misogynistic right from the very beginning of creation. Genesis 2:18 says, "The Lord God said, 'It is not good for the man to be alone. I will make a helper suitable for him.'"

Seeing the word "helper" with our twenty-first-century interpretive lens raises negative connotations of subservience and control. However, in the Old Testament, this word "helper" is most often used to describe God. God's people can declare that the Lord is "our help and our shield" (Psalm 33:20) and that "the Lord is with me; he is my helper" (Psalm 118:7). God comes alongside Israel as a "helper" to address her inadequacy.[1] In the same way, this Genesis account tells of woman being created to address man's inadequacy. The woman is not created to be a servant of man; rather, she is created to work alongside man as a co-laborer and companion in life.

While an explanation for the term "helper" can be provided quite cohesively, people often assert that the Bible is littered with tyrannical patriarchy that fundamentally discriminates against women. Is this true?

The idea that the Bible mandated a system of male oppression where women had no rights, freedom, responsibility, leadership, or autonomy can be contested from what we know from the Bible and from other external evidence sourced to date.[2]

Archaeology has been able to paint a picture for us of what household life looked like in ancient Israel and other related societies of that time. The household tasks of women and men overlapped in certain circumstances but were not the same. Women were responsible for what some gender archaeologists call "maintenance activities," used to describe the set of "practices and experiences concerning the sustenance, welfare, and long-term reproduction" of the household. These practices are the basic tasks of daily life. Many tasks required specialized knowledge and were essential in regulating and stabilizing both household and community life. These relevant responsibilities were broad and included economic, social, political, and religious activities.[3]

Economic activities were an integral part of household life in ancient Israel as in all agricultural societies. Women were largely responsible for food processing, textile production, and the fashioning of various household implements and containers including grinding tools, stone and ceramic vessels, baskets, weaving implements, and sewing tools. Many of these processes were not only time-consuming and physically demanding but also technologically sophisticated. On the whole, they likely required more technological skill than the tasks of men. The woman's role in commodity production was essential for household survival as ancient Israel probably lacked a developed market economy for most of the Iron Age. Ethnographic evidence strongly suggests that when women dominate indispensable household processes, they are positioned to exercise a considerable amount of household power and influence. For example, those responsible for preparing life-sustaining food would have a say in the household activities related to both production and consumption. They would also control allocation of household space and implements.[4]

CHAPTER 10: IS GOD A MISOGYNIST?

In short, depending on their age and experience, Israelite women had managerial roles, essentially functioning as the COOs (Chief Operating Officers) of their households. They were hardly oppressed and powerless, nor were they subordinate to male control in everyday life. In traditional subsistence societies comparable to ancient Israel, when women and men both made significant economic contributions to household life, female-male relationships were marked by interdependence or mutual dependence. Thus, the everyday workings in many marriages in ancient Israel (but not all) would have been viewed as a partnership. It seems that men dominated some aspects of household life and women others.[5]

Turning to biblical evidence now, a case can be made for the effective participation of Israelite women in professional positions within their wider communities. Their positions are quite numerous and varied, with some twenty different ones mentioned in the Hebrew Bible. We see a woman called Deborah operating as a judge within Israel.[6] Several royal women exercised political power as a *gebira* or "great lady."[7] Women contributed to the cultural realm as poets (Deborah, Miriam, Hannah, Lemuel's mother in Proverbs, the woman in Canticles) and performers in dance and music.[8] Religious roles carried out by woman included menial roles, for instance, the enigmatic women at the entrance to the tent of meeting;[9] cultic roles, for example, women along with male priests carried out a complex of ritual activities;[10] and authoritative roles, notably the female prophets—four named ones (Deborah, Miriam, Huldah, and Noadiah) and two unnamed women.[11]

Most of these professional women held considerable expertise and made significant contributions to their communities, with many carrying authority in their roles. They were hardly all dominated or controlled by male superiors. Further, those who worked within female cohorts or guilds (e.g., performers, lamenters, certain prophets) had their own hierarchies, with senior women or those with greatest expertise mentoring and teaching less-skilled women or apprentices.

To summarize here, I think that the evidence to date shows that to describe the Bible as operating within a realm of "tyrannical patriarchy" is a gross mischaracterization. Women within ancient Israel held important roles, responsibilities, and autonomy in their daily lives. However, let me be clear in stating that there was not gender equality in ancient Israel. For instance, Israelite patrilineality clearly favored men; a household's inheritance was transmitted across generations through male lines. This pattern underlies the male control of female sexuality that appears in biblical texts and also in ethnographic observations of traditional societies.[12]

Fast forward to the modern day, and I would suggest that there has never been a more favorable time to be a woman in the Christian church. In the church today, we find millions of women willingly and substantially participating on a daily basis. If I were to survey women that I have encountered in my church experience, I would confidently predict that the vast majority of them would testify to being equal to any man and treated as such the vast majority of the time. We, the church, are obviously not perfect and to be honest there are some pockets and aspects which could significantly lift their game. We don't have anywhere near enough women in church leadership and influence at the moment, and this is an area in which we must grow further. However, just like a woman can, in theory, become the CEO of a major publicly listed company, the same can be said within the church—and this is a good and right thing.

Despite this positive experience and all the positive evidence listed earlier, there are legitimate questions that remain around certain Bible messages that make for some difficult and downright disturbing reading in our culture today. Is the church following the true teachings and essence of Christianity regarding women, or has it just become more culturally appropriate as a matter of convenience?

Deuteronomy 22:28–29 says, "If a man happens to meet a virgin who is not pledged to be married and rapes her and they are discovered, he shall pay her father fifty shekels of silver. He must marry the young woman, for he has violated her. He can never divorce her as long as he lives."

At first reading, it appears the Bible is saying that a rapist should marry his

CHAPTER 10: IS GOD A MISOGYNIST?

victim, which is thoroughly disturbing. To interpret this passage properly, we must consider Exodus 22, which forms the backdrop to Deuteronomy 22.[13] Exodus 22:16–17 says, "If a man seduces a virgin who is not pledged to be married and sleeps with her, he must pay the bride-price, and she shall be his wife. If her father absolutely refuses to give her to him, he must still pay the bride-price for virgins."

In light of this Exodus reading, I think there are two possible interpretations for Deuteronomy 22:28–29.

Protectionist Reading

The protectionist interpretation argues that the passage is not condoning rape but is rather protecting the woman who has engaged in consensual sex with a man. You will rightly be puzzled at this point, so let me explain further.

There is some debate on whether the Hebrew word *taphas* should be translated "rape" in Deuteronomy 22:28. It can be argued that *taphas* reads softer in Hebrew than *chazaq*, which is translated "rape" in verse 25 of the same chapter. As highlighted in the previous chapter, biblical translation can be difficult because there are many more English words than ancient Hebrew words. However, translators have to make a decision, and it would appear in this instance that they've adopted the more conservative approach by using "rape" rather than watering down the translation with a lesser charge.

Let's assume for the moment that the translators got it wrong and they should have used "seduce" like the Exodus 22 counterpart. This verse now takes on a different complexion. In this ancient patriarchal context, if a virginal woman and a man engaged in consensual sex, and no marriage subsequently took place, then the woman would now be a very unattractive marriage prospect. This jeopardizes her long-term financial security and social status.

With this law in place, the following outcome can now be enforced:

- The man marries the woman and pays the bride price, with the man having no grounds for future divorce, or

- The man doesn't marry the woman but still pays the bride price

Whether or not the man marries the woman is dependent upon what the father and the daughter decide is in their best interests, which was the cultural custom of that day. The question of marriage is in their control entirely.

As such, it can be argued that this law adopts a *protective* disposition toward the woman. It would seem that the law is trying to eliminate the practice of men sleeping with whomever they want and subsequently damaging the financial prospects and social statuses of those women involved.

On the other hand, there is an alternative interpretation, which makes for harder analysis.

Plain Reading

Under this interpretation, the man has raped the woman and he essentially "gets away with it" by paying the bride price to the father. Under this interpretation, the following legal outcomes are the same as in the previous instance:

- The man marries the woman and pays the bride price, with the man having no grounds for future divorce, or
- The man doesn't marry the woman but still pays the bride price

It is highly unlikely that the first outcome would occur because the question of marriage is within the purview of the father and daughter to decide. It would be hard to imagine a father allowing his daughter to marry a rapist.

All that said, this interpretation and law just reek of injustice. Surely the man should receive a greater penalty then simply having to pay a financial penalty for rape. It is just plain wrong.

In terms of the likelihood of these two interpretations being correct, I lean toward the first protectionist reading. The second reading doesn't feel right for the following reasons:

1. If it is indeed talking about rape, then why wouldn't the same Hebrew

word be used in verse 28 as in the preceding commandment (verse 25, which used *chazaq* in the stronger form)?
2. The verse says if "they are discovered," rather than if "he is discovered," which implies that both are culpable.
3. This interpretation doesn't marry well with the greater weight of biblical evidence that views rape as an incredibly serious and utterly despicable act, which warranted the breaking out of war in some instances.

I appreciate that some of my more skeptical readers will think that I'm trying to wiggle my way out of this one. However, I would encourage those of you to keep an open mind as I outline the broader vein of biblical evidence that can speak to this subject on the whole.

In addition, I appreciate that there are other aspects of these passages that make for difficult reading in twenty-first-century society. The idea that a father controls the marriage rights of his daughter is one. However, as I mentioned at the start of this chapter, it's important to understand that the Bible can be descriptive and not only prescriptive. Just because it describes a practice doesn't mean it endorses that practice.

With that said, I'm going to turn to some more horrible biblical instances now that must be considered if we're going to answer the question of sexism in the Bible holistically.

> Then the Spirit of the LORD came on Jephthah. He crossed Gilead and Manasseh, passed through Mizpah of Gilead, and from there he advanced against the Ammonites. And Jephthah made a vow to the LORD: "If you give the Ammonites into my hands, whatever comes out of the door of my house to meet me when I return in triumph from the Ammonites will be the LORD's, and I will sacrifice it as a burnt offering."
>
> Then Jephthah went over to fight the Ammonites, and the LORD gave them into his hands. He devastated twenty towns from Aroer to the vicinity of Minnith, as far as Abel Keramim. Thus Israel subdued Ammon.
>
> When Jephthah returned to his home in Mizpah, who should come out

to meet him but his daughter, dancing to the sound of timbrels! She was an only child. Except for her he had neither son nor daughter. When he saw her, he tore his clothes and cried, "Oh no, my daughter! You have brought me down and I am devastated. I have made a vow to the Lord that I cannot break."

"My father," she replied, "you have given your word to the Lord. Do to me just as you promised, now that the Lord has avenged you of your enemies, the Ammonites. But grant me this one request," she said. "Give me two months to roam the hills and weep with my friends, because I will never marry."

"You may go," he said. And he let her go for two months. She and her friends went into the hills and wept because she would never marry. After the two months, she returned to her father, and he did to her as he had vowed. And she was a virgin.

From this comes the Israelite tradition that each year the young women of Israel go out for four days to commemorate the daughter of Jephthah the Gileadite. (Judges 11:29–40)

Another heartwarming story from the Old Testament! How on earth could a father sacrifice his only daughter? Words cannot suffice.

There are two possible interpretations of this passage that we need to consider.

Plain Reading

Jephthah vowed to offer a burnt offering to the Lord of whatever greeted him upon his return (v. 31). His daughter greeted him (v. 34). He then fulfilled the vow (v. 39). End of story.

Do Jephthah's actions communicate that God endorses child sacrifice? The Bible never condones child sacrifice, and it denounces the practice on many occasions.[14] Some make the argument that God does endorse the practice based on the story of Isaac and Abraham. As hard a read as this story is, Abraham never sacrificed Isaac; to make an argument that God's command equals endorsement is tenuous.

Could God have stopped Jephthah from fulfilling the vow? Potentially yes. Perhaps he tried to do so, but there is nothing in the text to suggest that he did. Does God's allowance of sacrifice equate to tacit approval of it? In many ways, this is what we explored in chapter 2 when we examined the question of suffering. As discussed, I don't think one can draw firm and conclusive views about the character of God based on this narrative given the existence of evil in our world.

Alternate Sacrifice Reading

Some scholars argue that Jephthah didn't perform a physical child sacrifice with his daughter.[15] Rather, they put forth that Jephthah devoted his daughter to a state of perpetual virginity.[16]

There is some merit to this argument. The text does seem to focus significantly on the girl's virginity, which seems out of place if this were to be a physical sacrifice. However, such an argument is not conclusive to many and this makes the text's interpretation hotly contested today.

Even if one were to read the text in this more positive light (perpetual virginity is preferable to death), this woman's sexuality is still being controlled by her father and this is demonstrably misogynistic.

What precisely to make of this story is a difficult question. It has numerous information gaps and is somewhat vague and evasive in nature. The author at no stage offers an assessment of Jephthah's conduct or his daughter's; nothing is said about what Yahweh makes of the events that transpire or the words that are spoken. The story is completely free of explicit value judgments.[17]

It certainly doesn't make matters any clearer that the book of Hebrews in the New Testament lists Jephthah as a hero of the faith.[18] While such an inclusion can't be taken to conclude that the Bible endorses his behavior in respect to his daughter, such a commendation doesn't help the case that God disapproved of this specific action, whether actual sacrifice or dedication. In summary, this story is a troubling one for which I can provide no substantial solace.

Prophetic Texts

Some of the prophetic writings of the Old Testament use "rape" language to depict God's impending judgment upon people and nations.[19] Skeptics of Christianity often reference these verses as evidence that the Christian God is misogynistic and inherently abhorrent.

In the first instance, we need to understand at a high level what the prophetic writings aim to do. Prophetic writings are written by "prophets." Prophets in ancient Israel were essentially the "mouthpieces of God," conveying God's opinions, reactions, intentions, and very words.

A lot of the language in the prophetic writings is poetic. It reads as shocking, and it is likely meant to be so. These prophets sought to get the attention of the people of Israel; using powerful imagery was one way to get it. The prophets often communicated that they wanted the people of Israel to be a holy people and to follow the ways of God rather than pursue their own agendas in life. To do otherwise was to incur the judgment of God, which—as the prophets articulated—was a deeply serious and consequential event.

Therefore, one should not view the "rape" language as God's endorsement of rape but rather his preparedness to expose the evils of humanity and to judge where necessary. To be concerned about the use of "rape" language here in this context is the equivalent of complaining about someone's aggressive bedside manner when they tell you that a tsunami is imminently approaching the shore. To be upset about the tone of delivery is to fundamentally not comprehend the severity and magnitude of the impending disaster.

I appreciate that there may be readers who are victims of rape who would have just found my assessment of this "rape" language insensitive. For this I am sorry; it is not my intention to make light of your pain. I want you to know that I believe in a God who sees you, weeps for you, and will judge for you.

We will now turn our attention to the New Testament writings, which on the whole are more positive than the Old Testament but still contain some thorny passages that require consideration.

CHAPTER 10: IS GOD A MISOGYNIST?

One such culturally jarring passage in the New Testament is 1 Timothy 2:11–14: "A woman should learn in quietness and full submission. I do not permit a woman to teach or to assume authority over a man; she must be quiet. For Adam was formed first, then Eve. And Adam was not the one deceived; it was the woman who was deceived and became a sinner."

We need to remember that the Bible, and more specifically the above passage, was not written to you and I in the twenty-first century. This passage was most probably written by the apostle Paul around the year AD 57 to his fellow worker Timothy who was ministering in Ephesus.[20]

Ephesus was an ancient Greek city located in modern day Turkey. Back in the day, the major religion in Ephesus centered around the Temple of Artemis, easily the biggest and largest temple in the city. There is much speculation by scholars about the specific religious practices that went on in the temple. Prominent New Testament scholar N. T. Wright suggests that it was a female-only led cult, and it was in this context that Paul issued his instructions to Timothy.[21]

We will probably not get a clear understanding of the exact context of Ephesus in our lifetime to make a concrete judgment on precisely what Paul was communicating here. If N. T. Wright is correct, then it can be argued that Paul was making a temporal instruction to Timothy because there were well-established female cult leaders in the city who were perhaps corrupting the new teachings of Jesus and others to suit their own agendas.

Another tough reading from the Bible is Ephesians 5:21–33:

> Submit to one another out of reverence for Christ.
>
> Wives, submit yourselves to your own husbands as you do to the Lord. For the husband is the head of the wife as Christ is the head of the church, his body, of which he is the Savior. Now as the church submits to Christ, so also wives should submit to their husbands in everything.
>
> Husbands, love your wives, just as Christ loved the church and gave himself up for her to make her holy, cleansing her by the washing with

> water through the word, and to present her to himself as a radiant church, without stain or wrinkle or any other blemish, but holy and blameless. In this same way, husbands ought to love their wives as their own bodies. He who loves his wife loves himself. After all, no one ever hated their own body, but they feed and care for their body, just as Christ does the church—for we are members of his body. "For this reason a man will leave his father and mother and be united to his wife, and the two will become one flesh." This is a profound mystery—but I am talking about Christ and the church. However, each one of you also must love his wife as he loves himself, and the wife must respect her husband.

This is jarring reading for us in the twenty-first century. It was jarring, too, for the ancient readers—albeit for very different reasons.

Since as early as the period of Aristotle, men have regarded women as an inferior species, and many women agreed with the sentiment.[22] Early Jewish teachers (e.g., Josephus, Philo) described women as inherently evil, holding little sense, and in need of subordination for their own good. At the more progressive end of the spectrum, the Greek philosopher Plutarch suggested that women could learn philosophy from their husbands; however, he based this suggestion on the premise that women would pursue folly if left to their own devices.[23] Imagine posting that on Twitter!

Given this cultural environment, it is not surprising that household codes of the time focused on instructing the household head on how to govern the members of his house. However, Paul's letter instructs the husband to love his wife. While such a practice was common, it was rarely prescribed.[24] This, in all probability, would have been quite jarring for all ancient hearers—male and female alike.

The jarring wouldn't have ended there. This appeal to the men to love their wives is formed on the model of Jesus loving his church. How did Jesus love his church? By ultimately laying down his life to be crucified on the cross. As Jesus did for the church, so should husbands do for their wives.[25] This is a staggering proposition for the men—especially in this cultural context!

I appreciate that some women will still find the direct instruction to "submit" insulting. However, we must appreciate Paul's instruction in a holistic sense. He was not giving instructions to husbands and wives on a mutually exclusive basis. Let's get really pragmatic here. Would a wife really have trouble submitting to a husband who loves her like Jesus loved the church? If this doesn't resonate with you, then I strongly encourage you to read the gospel books in the New Testament that recount the life and activities of Jesus. I really think you'll find them compelling.

Additionally, there is a broader vein of evidence from the apostle Paul that strongly indicates that he was a passionate advocate of women. In Paul's writings in the New Testament, he mentions forty helpers, of whom sixteen are women. Given the cultural context of the day, this should be considered an exceptionally high level of female participation, hardly becoming of a misogynist.[26]

So how did Jesus view women? Well, if I were making the case that he viewed them poorly, I would highlight the following:

1. Jesus did not have any formal female disciples. He had women who were part of his circle but none who were part of the "inner circle" (the twelve disciples).
2. In Mark 7, there is a story regarding a Syrophoenician woman whom Jesus calls a dog.

That's right, you heard me correctly.

On the other hand, there are many positive accounts of Jesus valuing women:

1. Jesus healed the mother-in-law of Simon Peter (a disciple of Jesus) of a fever (Matthew 8:14–15).
2. A woman touched Jesus's garment in a crowd of people and she was subsequently healed from a blood-hemorrhaging disorder (Mark 5:25–34).
3. Jesus healed the daughter of Jairus who was twelve years of age and on her deathbed (Mark 5:35–43).

4. Jesus saw a grieving widow mourning the death of her only son at his funeral. Jesus raised her son from the dead (Luke 7:11–17).
5. Jesus healed a woman who had been crippled by a spirit for eighteen years (Luke 13:10–17).
6. Jesus stood up for a woman who was being accused of adultery by the religious authorities of the day. Jesus's intervention resulted in the woman being freed (John 7:53–8:11).
7. Jesus engaged in conversation with a Samaritan woman at the well. In the Jewish world, to speak with a woman in public was heavily frowned upon, let alone to speak theology with her (John 4:1–42).
8. Several women were prominent followers of Jesus who traveled with him and the disciples, providing financial support for their ministry (Luke 8:1–3).
9. Another woman named Mary was taught by Jesus in the famous account of Mary and Martha. Martha expressed dismay because in that cultural context, a woman was not supposed to adopt a "learned" disposition. That was a man's place. Jesus, however, confirmed Mary's legitimacy as a student among the men, no doubt an eyebrow-raising moment in that day (Luke 10:38–42).[27]
10. The first witnesses and communicators of Jesus's resurrection were women. This is not to be dismissed as a minor detail. In those times, a woman's testimony was not considered valid in a court of law. The fact that Jesus chose to reveal himself to this group first would appear to be a symbolic act of defiance to a dysfunctional practice.

Clearly the case that I'm trying to mount here is that the weight of evidence points to Jesus being pro-women, but I appreciate that the instance of Jesus calling a woman a dog is quite surprising.

Scholars and commentators have speculated on the dog passage for years. It would seem highly unlikely given all the positive and countercultural interactions that Jesus had with women that Jesus was being sexist here. If anything, it could be better argued that Jesus was being racist in this instance; the term "dog" was a derogatory term used by Jews to describe non-Jewish people, and this woman was a Gentile.[28] Christian commentators generally skirt this awkward interaction by preferring to highlight the ultimate outcome of the back and forth: Jesus healed the woman's daughter. As important as that is, it still cannot be ignored that Jesus referred to this woman in a derogatory fashion. It cannot be passed off as some sort of "game" or "test" to elicit the woman's faith and devotion.[29] At this juncture, I must weigh this interaction in the context of all Jesus's other interactions with women.

While this interaction makes for a difficult reading, no serious scholar, historian, or average lay reader would conclude on the totality of the evidence that there is a material claim that Jesus was misogynistic or racist. The dog passage is the only troubling thorn in this whole debate and given my previous chapter's commentary regarding matters of translation and interpretation, I think it prudent to not rush off to firm conclusions on the basis of isolated and seemingly out-of-step evidence.

In conclusion, I think one can argue convincingly that the Bible articulates a progressive narrative of being pro-women within the cultural constructs of its time. God does not endorse patriarchal structures but rather has worked through them. Ultimately, the Bible reveals the ideal through the people of Jesus, Paul, and other biblical writers. That ideal is that women are equal, valued, and required to participate wholeheartedly and freely within society. Women can and must be confident in this. We, the church, can and must do better to foster an environment where such an ideal is the norm and not an aspiration.

CHAPTER 11

IS GOD A HOMOPHOBE?

For me, the norm growing up was that couples tended to live together prior to making any decision to marry. The wise thing to do was to see how the relationship endured everyday living arrangements, and if that went well, then perhaps marriage was the next appropriate step.

My wife and I were highly unusual in that we didn't do this. We made the reckless move of plunging straight into marriage without living together prior, and the primary motivation for doing so was our religious conviction. It won't come as a great surprise to many of you that Christian teaching prohibits premarital sex, and my wife and I respected this ideal.

All of the friends I had growing up knew that I held to this belief. They explicitly understood that I believed their personal actions in this respect to be immoral. This never led to any conflict in my relationships—except for the odd late-night religious debate, which was always done civilly. There wasn't any conflict because my friends probably thought my view was utterly ridiculous, archaic, and something of a legacy issue from my religious upbringing—ultimately not personally threatening to them in any way.

Fast forward to present day, and the question of homosexuality and the Christian faith elicits a vastly different tone of debate. I suspect that in all likelihood, homosexual relationships are immoral, and my view is abhorred by a significant portion of Western population today. Unlike the question of premarital sex, my view on homosexual relationships isn't just viewed as being ridiculous and archaic. My view is also considered highly offensive.

Why is my view on homosexual relationships judged so differently than my view on premarital sex? The answer goes to identity. When I say that I suspect homosexual relationships to be wrong, skeptics think I am saying that "homosexual people" are wrong. Their "innate nature" is wrong. Who they "are" is wrong. Homosexuality isn't just an act like premarital sex; it's a whole identity in its own right.

How, then, did a person's identity become so intensely entwined in their sexual preference? I can really only speculate, but I suspect that the Christian faith should probably shoulder some proportion of historical responsibility in this respect. I am not proud of how I have treated homosexuals in my lifetime. Whether it was playground insults, off-the-cuff remarks, or general insensitivity, I confess to being that ignoramus who followed the culture of my time rather than doing the hard work of putting myself in someone else's shoes and seeing the world from their perspective.

Given my historical behavior and society more generally, it seems that we may have unintentionally created a homosexual identity. Our insults and labels made people feel that their only defining feature was their sexuality. Their giftings and personality never made it into the fray. All that mattered was this one aspect about them. They were "gay," and "gay" wasn't cool (as defined by the masses).

I and society now have to live with the shame of knowing how our actions or lack thereof hurt people unnecessarily over the journey. How does one make up for it? I don't think one really can. We can have all sorts of LGBQTI groups within our workplaces where we go and wave our flags. However, that only further entrenches a person within these supposed identities, and I think this restricts the totality of who they really are.

So what does Christianity say to the homosexual community? Well, first, *it says sorry for the way that the church has historically treated the homosexual community.* As mentioned earlier, the Christian community has not always engaged with homosexual people in a way that is humane, curious, and empathetic. We can and must be better.

Second, and contrary to public understanding, *orthodox Christian doctrine does not condemn people to hell because they engage in homosexual sex*. I and others come to the table of Christianity with all our immorality and faults. Homosexuals do the same. One specific sexual act does not stand above all other acts in being able to condemn someone to hell.

Third, *I think the Christian God is not supportive of people engaging in homosexual sex or relationships*. Some Christians would disagree wholeheartedly on this view by saying that the Bible is gray and somewhat silent on the matter. However, I believe the narrative of the Bible is very clear and that it does not support homosexual sex or homosexual relationships.

This view begs the question: Why would God allow people to experience same-sex attraction yet not permit them to act on their desire? The short answer to this question is I'm not really sure. However, it is hardly an issue exclusive to homosexuals. All human beings experience desires in one form or another. Some are good, others not so good. A married man may desire another woman, but the mere fact that he desires her does not make it right to act on that impulse. *Desire, therefore, cannot automatically equate to legitimacy.*

Why it is that God seemingly gives us desires but forbids us from acting on them is a perplexing thing. However, my own experience has taught me that the so-called "rules" of God are good for my life. I have never regretted being a little bit more patient, a little bit more kind, or having one less beer—despite all of my desires to do the contrary. Maybe, just maybe, God knows what he is doing, and like a child submits to his or her parents, we are to do the same.

It is in this vein that Jesus asks us to follow him. When we kneel before him, he does not see us through the lens of sexual or any other earthly identity. He sees us as individually created by God, not one and the same, each with our own unique identity. It doesn't fundamentally matter whether one is Australian, gay, straight, black, or white. Our identity is not defined by these things, but rather by our creation in the very image of God, with each person carrying an infinite and equal amount of worth. Jesus asks all of us to find our identity in him, not in possessions, status, or sexuality. We must set all these things to one side if we are to follow his example. We are to be about his purposes and desires, not our own.

In summary, does God support homosexuality? I don't think so. Does God hate homosexual people? Absolutely not.

CHAPTER 12

WHAT ABOUT THE CRUSADES AND OTHER ATROCITIES?

I hear often that religion is the cause of all war. This is the preface to the idea that if religion is abolished, we'll see a lot less conflict in the world. Christianity literally has blood on its hands in its history. As much as Christians try to point to the person of Jesus as a loving, compassionate, and peaceful person, the Bible and history tell us a competing narrative. Is the essence of Christianity one of love, one of war, or some other combination? To explore this question further, we will need to take a closer look at some of the bloodshed that Christians have committed over the years. First, we'll look at the Crusades.

Crusades

The Crusades were military expeditions beginning in the late eleventh century that were organized by western European Christians in response to centuries of Muslim wars of expansion. Their objectives were to check the spread of Islam, retake control of the Holy Land in the eastern Mediterranean, conquer pagan areas, and recapture former Christian territories. There were approximately eight crusades in total, which took place from 1095 to 1291.[1] While no one can say with accuracy how many were slaughtered throughout the two centuries, estimates range from one to nine million people. To give this some perspective, at the upper estimate this represents 50 percent of the total population of Europe at the time.[2]

One of the worst chapters of the Crusades took place in 1099 when approximately ten thousand European Crusaders broke through the walls of Muslim-occupied Jerusalem. The Muslim inhabitants sought refuge in the Al-Aqsa Mosque, Islam's third holiest site, barricading themselves in. The European soldiers broke through and slaughtered thousands of men, women, and children, throwing some off the high walls and putting the rest to the sword. When the slaughter was over, the Crusaders marched to the nearby Church of the Holy Sepulchre—traditionally revered as the site of Calvary where Jesus was crucified—and held a thanksgiving service.[3]

There is much debate on what the primary motivations of the Crusaders were, whether they wanted to impose the Christian religion or were more imperialist in nature. I imagine these two things were intertwined during this period; however, the highly regarded Crusades scholar Jonathan Riley-Smith said the following about the motivations of the Crusaders:

> What characterizes it are an intense feeling that the actions are for God, the fact that at least the nucleus have to be volunteers, and they are performing their crusading duty as a penance.
>
> That penitential element, that feeling that you were actually engaged in a crusade to pay back to God for your sins, was so powerful, and remained in crusading for so long that even in the 15th and 16th centuries one can still see it.[4]

The key question then becomes: Are the actions of the Crusaders a true reflection of the essence of Christianity and how a Christian should live their life?

I would argue that there is never more intellectual and emotional tension than when discussing matters of war and Christian thought. In the Old Testament, we see God sanctioning warfare, and in the New Testament, Jesus instructs us to love our enemies and do good to those who hate us.[5] How does Christian thought reconcile these two seemingly opposing ideas?

The spectrum seems to have a warmonger at one end and a pacifist at the other. Nigel Biggar articulates the dilemma well:

> On the one hand going to war causes terrible evils, but on the other hand not going to war permits them. Whichever horn one chooses to sit on, the sitting should not be comfortable. Allowing evils to happen is not necessarily innocent, any more than actually causing them is necessarily culpable. Omission and commission are equally obliged to give an account of themselves. Both stand in need of moral justification.[6]

Crucial to shaping Christian thought on this dilemma was the fifth-century philosopher and bishop Augustine. He was broadly opposed to warfare but came to the view that under certain conditions, it could be appropriate for a Christian nation to go to war. The ideas he proposed initiated a "just war" tradition that has evolved via both theory and practice in the 1,500 years since. According to Augustine, wars should only be conducted in self-defense and with such a high regard for humanity that your enemy, if they lost, would not be left either humiliated or resentful. This a noble, albeit very difficult, outcome to achieve.[7]

Would the Crusades meet the criteria of a "just war"? Public intellectual and former archbishop of Canterbury Rowan Williams says of the compatibility between "just war" theory and the Crusades:

> Augustine is saying, "Look, things are falling apart. The world is pretty difficult. There are circumstances where you have got to do what isn't ideal. If, in order to fight off marauding barbarian tribes from northern Europe, you need to take to battle, well, all right, I suppose. I mean it's not a good thing, but the alternative is probably worse. And if you are going to do it and still remain some kind of a Christian, then for goodness' sake keep in mind the following moral principles. Nothing will make some behavior good." So it's a very grudging concession. It's certainly very different from the Crusader marching off to recover Jerusalem, shouting "God wills it."[8]

In summation, I don't think anyone can argue that the Crusades were truly reflective of the Christian way and how one should live their life as a Christian. The very idea that someone could "pay for their sins" by undertaking a holy war cannot be gleaned from the Bible nor from any of the early followers of Jesus and establishers of the Christian faith.

The Spanish Inquisition

It's a common quip in today's culture to describe being intensely questioned as undergoing a "Spanish Inquisition." The quip's origin owes itself to the practices undertaken by the newly unified Spanish kingdoms, through the period of 1478 to 1834, to identify religious heresies within its population.[9]

To set the scene, Spain became occupied by the Moors or Muslims, who ruled most of the Iberian Peninsula from the eighth century onwards. Christian states then began to recapture territory from the Moors, which ultimately led to the uniting of the Spanish crown in 1469 with the marriage of Ferdinand and Isabella from the kingdoms of Aragon and Castile, respectively. They became known as the Catholic Monarchs. The final conquest of the Moors was completed by Ferdinand and Isabella when they took control of Granada in 1492.

During this medieval period, Spain was the only multiracial and multireligious country in western Europe, with a large Jewish and Muslim population. Spanish Jews who converted to Christianity during this time became known as *conversos*. The *conversos* became a highly controversial group throughout Spain. Many of them and their descendants assumed important positions in government and society, aligning themselves with powerful noble families. They achieved economic power and prosperity, which led to them being resented by the "old Christians" who already questioned the sincerity of their conversions. In 1478, the Catholic Monarchs obtained a papal bull from Pope Sixtus IV, which set up the Inquisition to deal with the *conversos* whose conversions were thought to be fake.

So how did the Inquisition work? When the Inquisition opened an investigation in an area, they would visit the towns and make a proclamation that anyone engaging in Judaizing heresy had one month to submit themselves to the Inquisitors. In addition, people were invited to come forward if they

CHAPTER 12: WHAT ABOUT THE CRUSADES AND OTHER ATROCITIES?

knew of anyone who was engaging in heresy.[10] Inquisitors typically would offer relatively light penances to those who were willing to admit their own involvement in heresy. Those confessions were then used to identify other heretics who were brought before a tribunal. At this trial, the accused received no assistance to defend themselves and they were frequently ignorant of the charges against them. Confessions were often obtained through coercion, confiscation of property, or torture. If the accused were found guilty, the sentence would be announced at an auto-da-fé, which was an elaborate public spectacle. Then the accused would be handed over to the civil authorities who would carry out the sentence.

The three main methods of torture used by the Inquisition were:

1. *Garrucha* or pulley
2. *Toca* or water torture
3. *Potro* or rack

Garrucha (Pulley)

A quick way to bring on terrible distress and agonizing pain was the *garrucha*. The wrists of the accused were bound behind their back, and a rope tied to them was run through a pulley attached to the ceiling. Weights were attached to the victim's feet and they were hoisted upward and then allowed to fall back toward the ground, coming to a sudden halt. The severe jerk would often dislocate the arms and legs of the accused and would sometimes leave the individual permanently crippled.

Toca (Water Torture)

This involved placing the victim in a prone position on a wooden board with the head secured by an iron clamp. The nostrils of the nose were plugged and the jaws were forced open with a metal prong. A piece of linen cloth (*toca*) was then placed across the open mouth. Water was poured slowly on the cloth which gradually sank deeper and deeper into the throat while the prisoner experienced the terror of slow suffocation.

Potro (Rack)

This technique utilized a wooden frame with movable bars at each end. The prisoner's wrists and ankles were fastened to the bars, which were moved in opposite directions by levers. This would stretch the body until the bones separated. Those who experienced this ordeal sometimes never walked again. Those who fainted were revived and had the process repeated.

This is not one of the prouder chapters of the Christian tradition. All in all, it is estimated that thirty-two thousand individuals were executed under the Spanish Inquisition.

How could supposed Christians commit or allow such atrocities? It is difficult to judge precisely what the main drivers for the Inquisition were. It seems that it resulted from a combination of power consolidation and concern to maintain religious order in society, with these arguably working hand-in-hand. However, when one tries to analyze this atrocity, it is undeniable that the church played a primary role.

To be abundantly clear, the teachings of the Christian faith do not endorse anything remotely like the Spanish Inquisition. I cannot see how the Christian leaders of this period could genuinely believe that enforcing a religious view upon the general populace was somehow pleasing to God. Anyone who reads the books of Paul in the New Testament can plainly see a founding father who lovingly pleads, reasons, argues, and pursues the general populace to see the truth. Locking people up and torturing them is the antithesis of this.

Perhaps these leaders were concerned about the corrupting influence that these so called "heretics" would have on other Christians, so they acted for what they thought was the "greater good." All too often, history is littered with people and societies who rationalize their behavior to do whatever they want to do. I'm afraid to say that the Spanish Inquisition is probably one of those instances.

So far, I have touched on two higher profile instances of historical bad behavior by the Christian church, but sadly, as we all know, many more horrific acts have been committed by the Christian church. As the scholar David Bentley Hart states, "Not coincidentally, Christians are humans, and as a result tend to behave like human beings, as disappointing as that can be."[11]

So what does all this mean? Well, I want to make a couple of points.

First, Christian people need to be cognizant that Christians have done really horrible things in the name of God. As much as it is tempting for us to say, "They weren't really Christian," Jesus teaches us that we are to not judge others in that capacity. To say that someone is not a Christian on the basis of their works is to play the role of God as judge, and I think that is a very dangerous and arrogant disposition to adopt. Rather, we should presume that we are just as susceptible to failure as the Crusaders and Inquisitors and examine ourselves to see where our moral blind spots are today.

Second, perhaps you have suffered directly and severely because of the immoral actions of the Christian church. For that I am sorry. I earnestly ask that you focus your attention upon the character of Jesus, and it's my hope that you see in him what you haven't seen in the church.

Last, I would like to address those of you who are concerned that to adopt Christianity is to somehow subscribe to a culture that is divisive, combative, and archaic. The history of Christianity is mixed. Christians have done really good things, and they've done really bad things, with a whole lot of other stuff across the spectrum.

However, what is of primary importance to me is whether Christianity is objectively true in the first instance, and then second, whether that truth is any good. I have obviously come to that belief that it is true and that it represents an ultimate goodness that humanity should pursue. The Christian way is something akin to flying an A380. When it's flown according to the designer's instructions, it goes well. When it's not, the results are catastrophic.

CHAPTER 13

WHAT ABOUT OTHER RELIGIONS?

At the time of writing, this is the latest data pertaining to the religious persuasion of the world's population:

Table 10: World Religions and Their Representation[1]

Religion	Population	Percent
Christianity	2.3B	31.2
Islam	1.8B	24.1
Unaffiliated	1.2B	16
Hinduism	1.1B	15.1
Buddhism	0.5B	6.9
Folk religion	0.4B	5.7
Other religion	0.1B	0.8
Judaism	0.01B	0.2

As you can see, the majority of the world's population is not Christian. Is it, therefore, too narrow to say that people should follow one particular belief at the expense of all others? In this chapter, we'll explore whether exclusive truth claims are arrogant by nature and whether all religions have a role to play in contributing to overall truth.

To begin, I find that in Western culture, the average person is limited in their knowledge of major world religions. Let's take a brief flyover of the major three world religions—Islam, Hinduism, and Buddhism—to see what truth claims they make.

Islam

Islam is a monotheistic faith tradition that views itself as the culmination, completion, and correction of Judaism and Christianity. The word "Islam" means "surrender to God," and the word "Muslim" refers to an individual who "does Islam." In total, there are approximately 1.8 billion Muslims across the globe, representing many ethnicities, nationalities, and major language families.

Islam began in the early seventh century, officially beginning Islam's lunar calendar in AD 622. The faith originated in the west-central Arabian Peninsula region known as the Hijaz, within the city of Mecca. The foundational and central figure of Islam is Muhammad (c. AD 570 to 632), who was a son of a member of the Hashim clan of the Quraysh tribe. It is said that Muhammad received his commission as Prophet in AD 610 when he received his first auditory revelation from Allah (God).

The Quran is the principal text of Islam, comprising 114 chapters; it was delivered orally by Muhammad over some twenty-three years (AD 610 to 632) in the cities of Mecca and Medina.[2] For Muslims, the Quran is the word of God as revealed to and proclaimed by the Prophet Muhammad.

The core beliefs of Islam include the following:

1. Allah is the creator of all things.
2. Allah is the judge of all people.
3. Allah is the dispenser of recompense (paradise or hell).[3]

The core ritual practices of Islam are commonly referred to as the five pillars. They are as follows:

1. Profession of faith (shahada)
2. Five daily ritual prayers (salat)
3. Once in a lifetime pilgrimage to Mecca (haji)

4. Almsgiving (zakat)
5. Fasting (sawm, during lunar month of Ramadan)[4]

In respect to final judgment, all humans will one day be resurrected from the grave and brought before Allah and other witnesses. Based on the choices they have made during their lives, people are judged both as individuals and as groups. Their evil deeds will be weighed on a scale against their good deeds. People who find their deeds wanting will be sent down to the hellfire along with Satan. In hell, they will be guarded by the angel Malik and his nineteen angelic helpers whose task is to oversee their punishment. Those people who lived in submission to God will be sent up to paradise, envisioned as a garden of delights.[5]

Hinduism

Hinduism is the most geographically concentrated of all the major world religions; approximately 82 percent of the Indian population subscribes to Hinduism.[6] The current understanding of Hinduism as a world religion has come about only since the nineteenth century when Hindu reformers and Western orientalists came to refer to the diverse beliefs and practices that made up life in South Asia as "Hinduism." Hinduism has no one historical founder and no unified system of belief. There is no single doctrine of salvation and no centralized authority. In this sense, it is quite unique from other world religions. Diversity is a central feature of Hinduism, yet most scholars would agree that there are unifying strands that run through the diverse traditions of the faith.[7]

Although it is not easy to define Hinduism, we can confidently say that the following threads are shared by the majority of its adherents:

- Most Hindus believe in a Supreme God, whose qualities and forms are represented by the multitude of deities that originate from him.
- Hindus believe that human existence is a cycle of birth, death, and rebirth, governed by Karma.
- Hindus believe that the soul passes through a cycle of successive lives and its next incarnation always depends on how the previous life was lived.

- The main Hindu texts are the Vedas and their supplements (books based on the Vedas). Veda is a Sanskrit word meaning "knowledge." These scriptures do not mention the word "Hindu," but many scriptures discuss Dharma, which can be rendered as "code of conduct," "law," or "duty."[8]

According to the precepts of the faith, one does not become a Hindu; rather, one is born a Hindu.[9] For many of the faith, Hinduism is not so much a system of beliefs but a way of life.

Another prominent feature of Hinduism is the caste system. This system orders Hindu society hierarchically such that different social groups are ranked in relationships of superiority or inferiority to each other by their level of purity. Traditionally caste groups were largely occupational groups and your respective caste would determine most aspects of life, including your location of residence, social interaction, and who you could marry.[10]

Buddhism

Buddhism has its origins in the person of Siddhartha Gautama who lived in North India probably sometime in the fifth century BC. Siddhartha is said to have been born a prince who had a very privileged life free of suffering. However, when he encountered old age, sickness, and foresaw death, Gautama renounced his world of kingship and family. He then adopted the lifestyle of a "wandering seeker," which is not uncommon in Indian life. He sought the final truth that would lead to complete freedom from suffering. This involved a lot of meditation, study, and asceticism. All of this led Gautama to discover the truth or, as described another way, to "see it the way it really is." Experiencing this enlightenment set Gautama free, and he became the awakened one, the Buddha. Following his enlightenment, he gathered around him a group of followers who wandered all over North India teaching.[11] It is estimated that Gautama died in 483 BC.[12]

Buddhist tradition is unanimous that a creator God—in the sense that one is thought to exist by Christians—doesn't exist.[13] Rather the key theme of Buddhism is the elimination of suffering, not through material means but rather through seeing things the way they really are. In the Buddhist worldview, suffering is the result of our own ignorance and not understanding the way things really are. The way things really are at a foundational level is impermanent, meaning that all our experiences are non-fixed and subject to change. Suffering occurs when we endeavor to hold on to things in our lives and try to fix things down, so to speak. Being a Buddhist is all about learning how to let this desire go and see things for how they really are.[14]

There are Four Noble Truths within Buddhism:

1. The Truth of Suffering: No living being can avoid suffering (dukkha). Birth, sickness, senility, and death are all occurrences of suffering, whether physical or psychological.
2. The Truth of Origin: Suffering originates from excessive desire.
3. The Truth of Cessation: Suffering will cease when desire stops.
4. The Truth of the Eightfold Path: It is possible to stop desire, and hence suffering, by following eight principles of self-improvement.

The eight principles that make up the Eightfold Path are the following:

1. Right understanding (specifically of the Four Noble Truths)
2. Right thought (free of sensuous desire, ill will, and cruelty)
3. Right speech
4. Right conduct
5. Right livelihood
6. Right effort
7. Right mindfulness
8. Right meditation

All of these principles are equally important, and each is interdependent. None can be observed in isolation.[15]

In Buddhism, we are said to be an ever-flowing continuum of consciousness that continues from physical body to physical body in a process commonly referred to as rebirth. One's future body destination is subject to their good or bad deeds, commonly referred to as Karma. As such, suffering is never-ending; we are constantly being reincarnated and the process of "letting go" is constantly required to alleviate the suffering that life presents.[16]

Can suffering be let go once and for all? According to Buddhism, a state of nirvana can be achieved in a temporal sense when people who have cut off their Karma encounter a blissful state by ending desire, attachment, and ignorance. When one dies, they can potentially enter the final transpersonal state for eternity (commonly referred to as parinirvana), completely free from future rebirth.[17]

Reflections

In summary, I want to examine the original assertion that all of these worldviews have a contribution to make to the truth collective. From personal experience and my study of these faiths, I can see that these faiths do indeed offer many benefits and are valid in many ways. For instance, in respect to Islam, I greatly appreciate that Muslims live out of daily disciplines and cultivate strong communities the world over. I feel that I and many of my fellow Christians would benefit greatly from learning from our Muslim brothers and sisters in this respect.

In a similar sense, Hinduism has a strong sense of community and belonging. I also think that belief in Karma can be something of a fillip in our world where we consistently need social justice to be enacted more and more.

In Buddhism, I love the contemplative aspects where one is to take a step back to give perspective to their existence, the suffering they endure, and how they are to make sense of it all.

I could see myself adopting all of these practices and reaping the benefits for myself and others.

I've heard it said before that the religious pursuit of God is something akin to a group of blind men attempting to describe an elephant. One man touches the trunk and says that it resembles a snake. Another touches a leg and describes it as a tree trunk. The next touches the ear and says it is like a large tree leaf. And so on and so forth. The purpose of the story is to convey that each individual religion can only ascertain a part of the truth and never the whole truth.

At first hearing, this analogy makes sense. What we easily miss in this story, though, is that someone sees the whole elephant. Who is that person? Is it you or I? If it is, then why do you and I have the capacity to see the whole truth when others can't? Can you see the problem here? The analogy is originally told to make the point that no one person can see the whole truth, but the analogy is self-defeating because someone must *see the whole truth* to communicate the analogy.

If we can then proceed on the basis that it is possible for someone to have a greater grasp of the truth than another, how does the Christian faith primarily distinguish itself and lay claim to being "the truth" over the other world religions?

The answer lies in the daily lived experiences of the faiths. With Buddhism, Islam, and Hinduism, it's all about doing. It's primarily about being good, thinking right, and perfecting your religious practices. If you reach a certain level of performance, then you will gain access to God, heaven, or nirvana, depending on your persuasion.

What exactly constitutes that certain level of performance is a vexed question. The Christian faith distinguishes itself here in that it says that there is nothing you can do to earn relationship with God. Say you were 99 percent perfect in all that you did and said. In the Christian worldview, that doesn't pay the admission price to gain access to a God who is 100 percent pure in all manner and form.

The good news in Christianity is that there is no admission price. But there are admissions: An admission that God exists and he is 100 percent perfect. An admission that you are a broken person who is never capable of being in the same room as God in your own strength and works. An admission that Jesus Christ lived and walked this earth, and ultimately died and rose again three days later. An admission that his death and resurrection was not a party trick but enables you to be in the same room with God because it deals with your sin and brokenness once and for all.

For some of you, this is all a terrifying prospect. The idea of yielding to the knowledge that you are incapable of repairing yourself is paradoxical to the way you have lived your life to date. The pursuit of wealth, love, and status have gone some way to giving you the self-worth that you desire. I imagine that to admit that those efforts have been futile is a hard thing to do.

The good news is that those efforts haven't been futile. Despite the PR of God and Christianity in general, God wants you to live a fulfilling life, which includes fruitful and enjoyable work, loving and meaningful relationships, and the broader enjoyment of this planet and all it has to offer. Choosing to follow God will probably mean that all of this good stuff will get to continue, albeit in a somewhat different light.

In summary, I don't think all religions can be lumped in one basket and labeled as "valid." Upon examination, they all make very different truth claims, in essence are very different, and need to be evaluated in their own right. To suggest that Christianity is arrogant because it makes exclusive truth claims is self-defeating. This is because one must rely upon the premise that no one person can have the truth, which is a truth claim. And if one can make that truth claim without arrogance, then perhaps others can do likewise.

CHAPTER 14

IF I REFUSE AM I GOING TO HELL?

The term "hell" is somewhat lost in our culture today. In our everyday vernacular, it is a casual throwaway line with a "go to hell" or "what the hell." When people like Josef Fritzl come into our purview, we desire and welcome hell's existence. Other times, it feels like an incredibly antiquated idea that serious thinkers shouldn't waste any time or attention on. This little nomadic four-letter word really struggles to find a place to lay its head in our world of Western thinking.

When we think of hell, we generally imagine a place that fits the stereotype: rampant devils abounding in a fire-laden, destitute landscape. For a lot of us, this imagery doesn't help us take the concept seriously. It all sounds ludicrous and just pretty silly. However, despite these feelings, I find that time and time again, serious and intelligent people wonder about the concept of hell and are somewhat concerned about its potential existence.

So what did Jesus have to say about the subject? Let's take a look at the following sayings of Jesus, which will give us a flavor of his thoughts:

- Then he will say to those on his left, "Depart from me, you who are cursed, into the eternal fire prepared for the devil and his angels. For I was hungry and you gave me nothing to eat, I was thirsty and you gave me nothing to drink, I was a stranger and you did not invite me in, I needed clothes and you did not clothe me, I was sick and in prison and you did not look after me." They also will answer, "Lord, when did we see you hungry or thirsty or a stranger or needing clothes or sick or in prison, and did not help you?" He will reply, "Truly I tell you, whatever you did not do for one of the least of these, you did not do for me." Then they will go away to eternal punishment, but the righteous to eternal life. (Matthew 25:41–46)

- But I tell you that anyone who is angry with a brother or sister will be subject to judgment. Again, anyone who says to a brother or sister, "Raca," is answerable to the court. And anyone who says, "You fool!" will be in danger of the fire of hell. (Matthew 5:22)
- You snakes! You brood of vipers! How will you escape being condemned to hell? (Matthew 23:33)
- Then he left the crowd and went into the house. His disciples came to him and said, "Explain to us the parable of the weeds in the field." He answered, "The one who sowed the good seed is the Son of Man. The field is the world, and the good seed stands for the people of the kingdom. The weeds are the people of the evil one, and the enemy who sows them is the devil. The harvest is the end of the age, and the harvesters are angels. "As the weeds are pulled up and burned in the fire, so it will be at the end of the age. The Son of Man will send out his angels, and they will weed out of his kingdom everything that causes sin and all who do evil. They will throw them into the blazing furnace, where there will be weeping and gnashing of teeth. Then the righteous will shine like the sun in the kingdom of their Father. Whoever has ears, let them hear…. This is how it will be at the end of the age. The angels will come and separate the wicked from the righteous and throw them into the blazing furnace, where there will be weeping and gnashing of teeth." (Matthew 13:36–43, 49–50)
- I say to you that many will come from the east and the west, and will take their places at the feast with Abraham, Isaac and Jacob in the kingdom of heaven. But the subjects of the kingdom will be thrown outside, into the darkness, where there will be weeping and gnashing of teeth. (Matthew 8:11–12)
- If your hand causes you to stumble, cut it off. It is better for you to enter life maimed than with two hands to go into hell, where the fire never goes out. (Mark 9:43)
- I tell you, my friends, do not be afraid of those who kill the body and after

that can do no more. But I will show you whom you should fear: Fear him who, after your body has been killed, has authority to throw you into hell. Yes, I tell you, fear him. (Luke 12:4–5)

And finally, I want to share this story that Jesus told in Luke 16:19–31:

> There was a rich man who was dressed in purple and fine linen and lived in luxury every day. At his gate was laid a beggar named Lazarus, covered with sores and longing to eat what fell from the rich man's table. Even the dogs came and licked his sores.
>
> The time came when the beggar died and the angels carried him to Abraham's side. The rich man also died and was buried. In Hades, where he was in torment, he looked up and saw Abraham far away, with Lazarus by his side. So he called to him, "Father Abraham, have pity on me and send Lazarus to dip the tip of his finger in water and cool my tongue, because I am in agony in this fire."
>
> But Abraham replied, "Son, remember that in your lifetime you received your good things, while Lazarus received bad things, but now he is comforted here and you are in agony. And besides all this, between us and you a great chasm has been set in place, so that those who want to go from here to you cannot, nor can anyone cross over from there to us."
>
> He answered, "Then I beg you, father, send Lazarus to my family, for I have five brothers. Let him warn them, so that they will not also come to this place of torment."
>
> Abraham replied, "They have Moses and the Prophets; let them listen to them."
>
> "No, father Abraham," he said, "but if someone from the dead goes to them, they will repent."
>
> He said to him, "If they do not listen to Moses and the Prophets, they will not be convinced even if someone rises from the dead."

While Jesus hasn't mentioned anything resembling demons with pitchforks, you can see that he consistently used strong and terrifying language to describe hell. For him, hell is characterized by suffering, fire, darkness, and lamentation.[1]

There has been no consensus reached within Christian scholarship on the precise nature of hell. Some say it is a physical place with everlasting torment, while others say it is temporal state that ultimately results in annihilation of the soul. I think to spend too much time debating such things distracts from Jesus's primary point. Jesus speaks of something called hell, and it's clearly not a great place to be. He wants us to take it very, very seriously.

People often ask me who I think ends up in hell. I don't think anyone can or should answer this question definitively. It is not up to you and I to tell someone whether they are going to hell or not. I believe that when Jesus speaks of hell, he is speaking to us as individuals. I do feel that I am personally deserving of hell. When confronted face to face with a holy God, I am not worthy of anything other than complete separation from him if I have made no effort to pursue him in this lifetime in the manner he desires.

Some of you may feel that you are worthy and that for God to not accept you just as you are, without pursuit of him whatsoever, makes God an immoral monster. The concept of judgment as I see it played out in today's society seems to have an internal contradiction. Many would view this book as "judgmental" and thus inherently "wrong." However, that view in itself is a judgment, and if judging is wrong, then that assessment must be wrong too.

The purpose of all this intellectual tongue twisting is to make the point that there is nothing inherently wrong with God being judgmental. What ultimately matters is whether one is fair in their judgment. Let's say that after reading this book you decide that the message of Christianity and the cross really isn't for you. You live your life and, by many people's standards, you've become a pretty good moral person in nearly all of life's dealings. Your eventual death arrives, you stand face to face with God, and he refuses to let you through the pearly gates. Is that fair?

It could be argued no. How could God say no to this person, yet admit a serial rapist who simply accepted the forgiving work of Jesus Christ on his deathbed? I personally was fortunate enough to grow up in a quality environment. I was raised by two loving parents who provided for me in all ways. I received a high quality education. I have always had access to high quality drinking water, food, and health care. I am deemed by most to be a reasonably moral person.

As much as I would love to attribute all of my moral behavior to my own sheer personal determination, we all know this is simply a lie. All of us to an extent are products of our surroundings, and the majority of us know that people who commit atrocious crimes predominantly haven't had the privilege of a good upbringing. Is it right that God dismisses them and accepts me?

The extent to which someone is responsible for their actions is a complex dilemma. To one extreme, we can absolve ourselves of any responsibility and blame our circumstances for the actions we commit. To think of how the world would look if we adopted such an abolitionist disposition isn't an attractive prospect to most, I would imagine. At the other extreme, a regime so harsh that no one could live out a day without falling foul of the judicial system would embed guilt into every nook and cranny of our world and being. This is hardly a viable alternative.

It seems that where society has ultimately settled is that the majority of people must be treated as beings with a capacity for judgment, a capacity to choose between good and evil, and not capable of always getting it right. In a similar vein, the God of Christianity asks us to humbly acknowledge our personal agency and shortcomings. This seems to me to be the most fair and reasonable of expectations, to acknowledge that we as individual people are not perfectly finished articles; we are in need of some fixing.

Despite all of my attempted rationalizations here, I appreciate that some of us will feel that God is playing some twisted game at our expense. Al Pacino's character in *The Devil's Advocate* describes this attitude well:

> Let me give you a little inside information about God. God likes to watch. He's a prankster. Think about it. He gives man instincts. He gives you this extraordinary gift and then what does he do? I swear,

for his own amusement, his own private cosmic gag reel. He sets the rules in opposition, it's the goof of all time. Look, but don't touch. Touch, but don't taste. Taste, but don't swallow. And while you're jumping from one foot to the next, what is he doing? He's laughing his sick, f****** ass off. He's a tightass, he's a sadist. He's an absentee landlord. Worship that? Never![2]

I think if we're honest we can all empathize with this rant. At so many points in our human existence, we can relate to the difficulties involved in doing the right thing. If instituted by God, this all can seem rather unfair and egocentric.

The thing we have to remember with the rant, however, is that it assumes that God does exist and is responsible for this supposedly unfair system. And at the end of the day, can we be so confident, so assured, that we can wave a finger in God's face and say "not good enough"?

Perhaps it's time for a little bit of poetry from the Bible. The Lord says to Job in Job 38:

> Who is this that obscures my plans with words without knowledge? Brace yourself like a man; I will question you, and you shall answer me.
>
> Where were you when I laid the earth's foundation? Tell me, if you understand. Who marked off its dimensions? Surely you know! Who stretched a measuring line across it? On what were its footings set, or who laid its cornerstone—while the morning stars sang together and all the angels shouted for joy?
>
> Who shut up the sea behind doors when it burst forth from the womb, when I made the clouds its garment and wrapped it in thick darkness, when I fixed limits for it and set its doors and bars in place, when I said, "This far you may come and no farther; here is where your proud waves halt"?

And here is the crux of the matter: Who knows better? God or you? Will you trust in the God of the universe and concede that perhaps you don't know its exact dimensions? Or will you trust your own path? I think C. S. Lewis says it well: "There are only two kinds of people in the end: those who say to God, 'Thy will be done,' and those to whom God says, in the end, 'Thy will be done.' All that are in Hell, choose it. Without that self-choice there could be no Hell. No soul that seriously and constantly desires joy will ever miss it. Those who seek find. To those who knock it is opened."[3]

My first preference is that you choose Christianity because it's true and because it will give your life the fullest purpose, spice, and meaning. It has been my hope that this book has been effective in making the case for this view, and it's on that pedestal that you can choose to follow the teachings of Jesus Christ in full confidence. However, in the possibility that I have not been successful in this, I have had to disclose fully Jesus's teachings on hell. It is the only loving thing to do.

CHAPTER 15

WHERE TO FROM HERE?

Perhaps you've followed your way through this book, and you're now at a position where you are actually considering the Christian faith. It is a jarring position, one where you may find yourself "in too deep" in respect to many of the intellectual aspects of the faith, yet seriously uncertain and fearful of what consequences such an intellectualization may lead to in your everyday life.

It's a completely understandable position, and I can possibly relate to where you are at this minute. You may be asking, "Drew, say I were to commit to becoming a Christian, to sign on the dotted line, what does that mean for my daily life? What are the rules that I need to follow?"

Well, first, let's revisit what I defined Christianity to be in the preface.

A Christian is someone who believes the following:

1. God created the universe and everything in it.
2. God created human beings with a capacity to relate to him, as distinct from other creatures.
3. As human beings, we consistently fall short of the best that God intends for us and our world, which creates a gap between us and God.
4. Through belief in the death and resurrection of Jesus Christ, we can bridge this gap to God once and for all.
5. God then wants to be intimately involved in our lives, helping you and I to bring about a better world where justice, peace, and prosperity reign for all.

At this point, I want you to review what you wrote about these claims at the start of this book. Do you still agree with your thoughts and sentiments now?

Being a Christian is not about whether you go to church or not. Being a Christian is not about becoming Mother Teresa overnight either. It is about submitting your heart to the person of Jesus Christ, accepting who he is and what he did for you on the cross—namely, bridging the gap of sin and death between you and him once and for all.

In my experience, when people make the decision to accept Jesus and to involve him in their lives, things start to change. Where they may have derived joy and meaning in the past from their relationships, jobs, money, or whatever it may be, they now start to view all of these things through the filter of the person of Jesus. For some people, that may mean they get out of a particular relationship. For others, it may mean they begin to work harder on that relationship and invest more to improve it. Some people will change their jobs; others will work harder in theirs. Some may even start going to church. Ordinarily, such changes may seem ridiculous and impossible. However, when someone realizes who Jesus really is, then this will inevitably change the way they view everything. Perhaps that process has already started for you through this book.

Let's for a moment assume that after reading this book you're still not in agreement with all the tenets listed above. As such, you will probably not be prepared at this point to make a decision to become a Christian. First, I want to say thank you for being open-minded and taking the time to read this book. Second, I'd love to hear your thoughts and criticisms about the book in greater detail. You can email me at drew@honestchristianity.org.

On the other hand, let's for a moment assume that you are now in agreement with some of the above statements. However, you are still unprepared to make a decision to become a Christian. At this point I want to thank you, too, for taking the time to read this book, and I'd love to hear your thoughts as well.

Lastly, let's for a moment assume that you are now in agreement with all of the above and you do want to make a decision to become a Christian.

I, of course, think that is outstanding news. The process of becoming a Christian is fantastically simple. You don't need to seek out a religious guru, although in some cases that can be helpful. You see, as explained, in previous chapters, becoming a Christian is a matter of the head and the heart. It's about coming to a place of recognition and acceptance of who the person of Jesus was and is. To become a Christian, you need to accept that the work of Jesus related to you and to you alone, and make a commitment that you will follow his teaching and guidance moving forward. Obviously, all of us fail in following Jesus "perfectly" in all things, but what is important is that we accept that his death and resurrection covers our ineptitude and compels us to try to follow his example in all things. So, with that said, if you want to become a Christian, please say the following prayer to God:

> *Dear Lord Jesus, I know that I am a sinner, and I ask for your forgiveness. I believe you died for my sins and rose from the dead. I turn from my sins and invite you to come into my heart and life. I want to trust and follow you as my Lord and Savior. May my life now be about your purposes and pursuits. In your name I pray. Amen.*

If you just said that prayer for the first time, then I'd love to hear from you. Saying that prayer is a big deal, and I want to put you in touch with people in your area who can provide some guidance and support in this new life decision. God intends for us to do life alongside others who help and encourage us, and I want to give you that opportunity to connect with others.

I promise you won't end up in a convent in the mountains chanting songs. The people I will connect you with are relatively normal people, and I'm confident you'll see that pretty quickly.

Thanks again for investigating. I pray that God uses you mightily in all facets of your life to bring about a better world for all.

Take care.

APPENDICES

Appendix 1: Kings Chronology

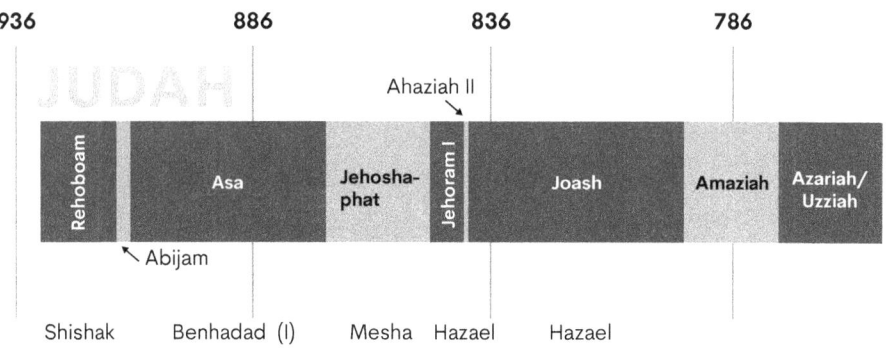

This timeline shows the chronological reigns of Judaean and Israeli rulers as communicated by the Old Testament. The listing of foreign rulers inward of both timelines each represent an Old Testament reference to when that foreign ruler was ruling.

In summary, this timeline order is impeccably accurate as evidenced by external sources. This adds significant credibility to the argument that the relevant biblical passages are communicating accurate data.

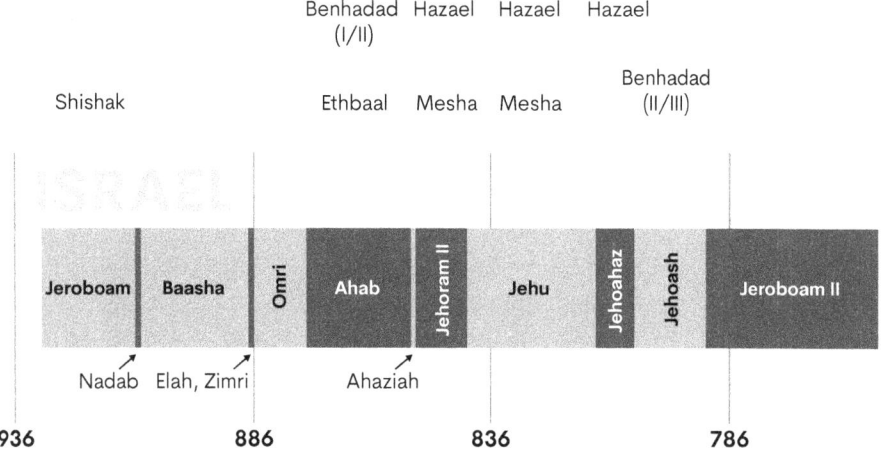

APPENDIX 1: KINGS CHRONOLOGY

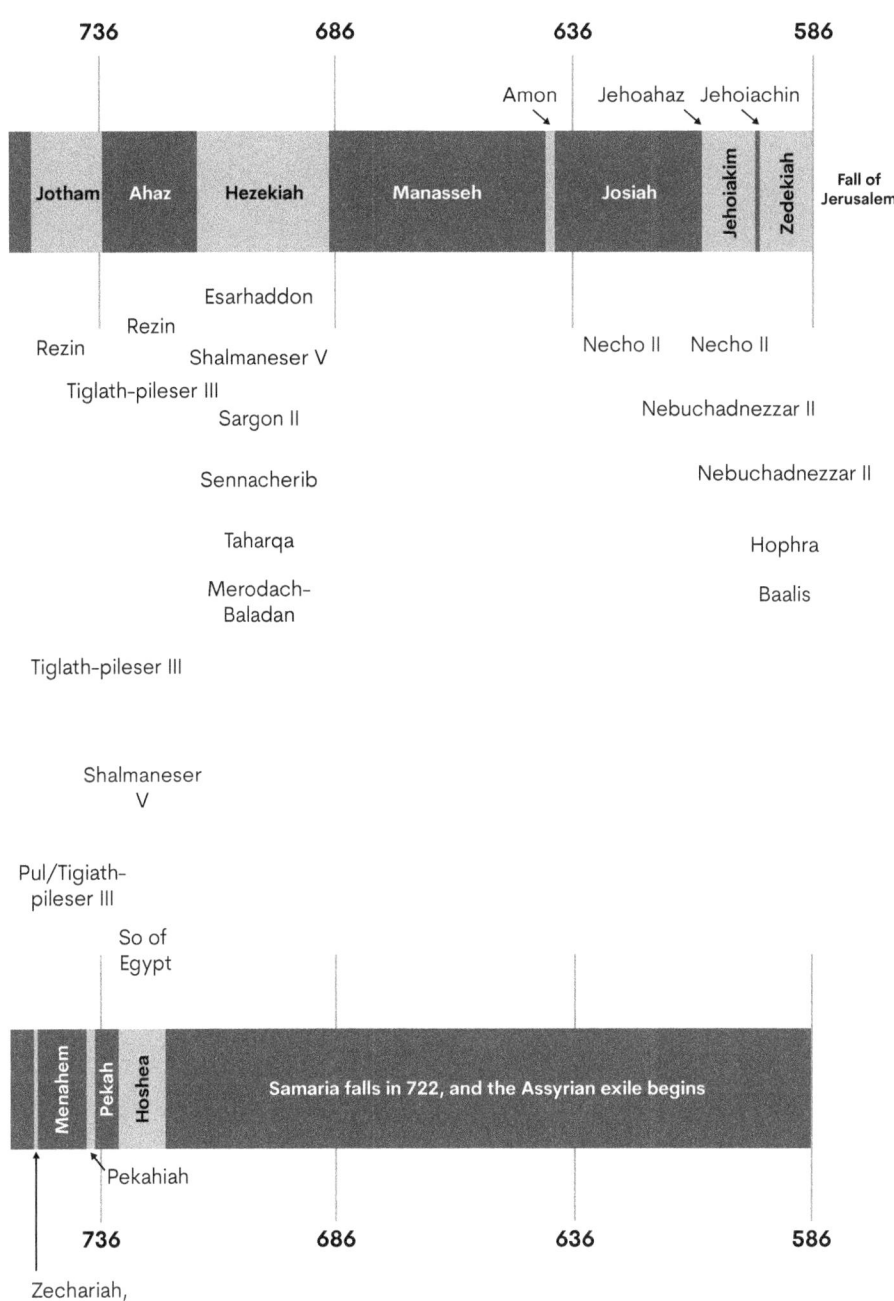

Appendix derived from Kitchen, On the Reliability of the Old Testament, 7-64.

Appendix 2: The Apocrypha

Title	Estimated Date of Authorship	Description
First Esdras	2nd century BC[1]	First Esdras is a historical account of Israel from the eighteenth year of King Josiah to the time of Ezra. It forms a parallel history to sections of Chronicles and Ezra-Nehemiah.[2]
Second Esdras	By AD 100 latest[3]	A collection of three apocalyptic texts[4] written after the destruction of the second temple (AD 70).[5]
Tobit	Early 2nd century BC[6]	Regarded predominantly as a fictional work centered upon the primary character of Tobit, written for didactic edification.[7]
Judith	By AD 100 latest[8]	Regarded as fictious work[9] centered upon the heroic and beautiful Jewish widow Judith.[10]
Additions to Esther	By AD 93/94 latest[11]	Additions to the traditional Hebrew book of Esther are comprised of: 1. Mordecai's dream and the plot of the two eunuchs against the king 2. The text of the king's edict authorizing the destruction of Persian Jewry 3. The prayers of Mordecai and Esther 4. Esther's approach to the king 5. The edict reversing the decree of destruction 6. The interpretation of Mordecai's dream, followed by the colophon[12]
The Wisdom of Solomon	1st century BC[13]	Most probably written to the Jewish diaspora community of Alexandria (chief city of Hellenistic and Roman Egypt), the book advocates resistance to cultural assimilation and defends Jewish monotheism and morality.[14] The book is commonly attributed to King Solomon, but it was actually written in the time of the early Roman Empire, probably by a Greek-educated Jew.[15]

APPENDIX 2: THE APOCRYPHA

Title	Estimated Date of Authorship	Description
Ecclesiasticus (Wisdom of Sirach)	200 to 175 BC[16]	A book of wisdom literature containing practical guidance, prayers, and poetry. Authorship is attributed to Ben Sira; the prologue of the book claims that his grandson moved to Egypt in 132 BC and subsequently translated the work into Greek.[17]
Baruch	2nd century BC to AD 70[18]	Named after Baruch who was the secretary to the Old Testament prophet Jeremiah.[19] This work purports to be a letter sent by Baruch to members of the Jerusalem community who had not been exiled. The book appears to contain several historical errors.[20]
Susanna (addition to Daniel)	Before 100 BC[21]	A story of the eventual vindication of an innocent woman who escaped an attempted rape by two of the elders of the community. Generally regarded to be non-historical and folkloric in nature.[22]
Bel and the Dragon (addition to Daniel)	Before 100 BC[23]	A story of two interwoven court tales that are principally polemical parodies of idolatry.[24] Daniel exposes the priests of the idol Bel as frauds and then he kills a great dragon. As a result, he is thrown into a den of lions, which do not harm him, and he is eventually released.[25]
The Prayer of Azariah and the Song of the Three Jews (addition to Daniel)	Before 100 BC[26]	A two-part work comprised of a prayer of confession and plea for mercy, followed by a lengthy and elaborate hymn of praise.[27]
The Prayer of Manasseh	Before 100 BC[28]	A prayer that claims to have moved God to forgive the wicked king of Judah (Manasseh) and restore him from his captivity in Babylon to his throne in Jerusalem (2 Chronicles 33:12–13).[29]

Title	Estimated Date of Authorship	Description
First Maccabees	100 BC[30]	A historical account of political, military, and religious observances centered upon three generations of the Jewish Maccabeus family, covering the period of 169 to 134 BC.[31]
Second Maccabees	1st century BC[32]	A separate book to 1 Maccabees, this historical account supplements the history of the first book starting in 180 BC during the reign of Seleucus IV and concluding in 161 BC with the victory of Judas the Maccabee over the enemy general Nicanor.[33]
Third Maccabees	217 BC to AD 70[34]	This book has no relation to the other three books of Maccabees. It recounts events that supposedly took place in the reign of the Hellenistic king of Egypt, Ptolemy IV (221 to 204 BC), with most of the book focusing its attention on Ptolemy's vicious persecution of the Jews in Egypt.[35]
Fourth Maccabees	Middle half of the 1st century AD[36]	A philosophical treatise composed in Greek, which proclaims that reason is always superior to the emotions and that reason is compatible with the Mosaic law. To make its case, the book retells the martyrdom stories of Eleazar and of the seven sons with the mother from 2 Maccabees.[37]
Psalm 151	520[38] to 100 BC[39]	An "additional" psalm to the traditional 150 that describes various aspects of the life of David and "is ascribed to David as his own composition." It covers his work as a shepherd, his musical ability, his selection by God even though his "brothers were handsome and tall," and his victory over Goliath.[40]

Below is a statue by the great Italian sculptor Donatello, depicting the moment of Judith beheading Holofernes as described in the Apocrypha book of Judith.

Figure 20. Judith and Holofernes by Donatello –
Located outside the Palazzo Vecchio, Florence Italy
Credit: Foxycha/Shutterstock.com. Used with permission.

Appendix 3: Old Testament Collections

	Tanakh		Josephus		Protestant Bible
Pentateuch	1 scroll	Genesis	1 scroll	Genesis	Genesis
	1 scroll	Exodus	1 scroll	Exodus	Exodus
	1 scroll	Leviticus	1 scroll	Leviticus	Leviticus
	1 scroll	Numbers	1 scroll	Numbers	Numbers
	1 scroll	Deuteronomy	1 scroll	Deuteronomy	Deuteronomy
Nevi'im	1 scroll	Joshua	1 scroll	Job	Joshua
	1 scroll	Judges	1 scroll	Joshua	Judges
	1 scroll	Samuel	1 scroll	Judges	Ruth
	1 scroll	Kings		Ruth	1 Samuel
	1 scroll	Isaiah	1 scroll	Samuel	2 Samuel
	1 scroll	Jeremiah	1 scroll	Kings	1 Kings
	1 scroll	Ezekiel	1 scroll	Isaiah	2 Kings
	1 scroll	Hosea	1 scroll	Jeremiah	1 Chronicles
		Joel		Lamentations	2 Chronicles
		Amos	1 scroll	Ezekiel	Ezra
		Obadiah	1 scroll	Hosea	Nehemiah
		Jonah		Joel	Esther
		Micah		Amos	Job
		Nahum		Obadiah	Psalms
		Habakkuk		Jonah	Proverbs
		Zephaniah		Micah	Ecclesiastes
		Haggai		Nahum	Song of Songs
		Zechariah		Habakkuk	Isaiah
		Malachi		Zephaniah	Jeremiah
Ketuvim	1 scroll	Psalms		Haggai	Lamentations
	1 scroll	Proverbs		Zechariah	Ezekiel
	1 scroll	Job		Malachi	Daniel
	1 scroll	Song of Songs	1 scroll	Psalms	Hosea
	1 scroll	Ruth	1 scroll	Proverbs	Joel
	1 scroll	Lamentations	1 scroll	Song of Songs	Amos
	1 scroll	Ecclesiastes	1 scroll	Ecclesiastes	Obadiah
	1 scroll	Esther	1 scroll	Daniel	Jonah
	1 scroll	Daniel	1 scroll	Chronicles	Micah
	1 scroll	Ezra	1 scroll	Ezra	Nahum
		Nehemiah		Nehemiah	Habakkuk
	1 scroll	Chronicles	1 scroll	Esther	Zephaniah
					Haggai
					Zechariah
					Malachi

APPENDIX 3: OLD TESTAMENT COLLECTIONS

Catholic Bible	Orthodox Bible	Apocrypha
Genesis	Genesis	1 Maccabees
Exodus	Exodus	2 Maccabees
Leviticus	Leviticus	3 Maccabees
Numbers	Numbers	4 Maccabees
Deuteronomy	Deuteronomy	Judith
Joshua	Joshua	Tobit
Judges	Judges	Ecclesiasticus or the Wisdom of Jesus Son of Sirach
Ruth	Ruth	The Wisdom of Solomon
1 Samuel	1 Kingdoms (comprising 1 Samuel)	Prayer of Manasseh
2 Samuel	2 Kingdoms (comprising 2 Samuel)	Baruch
1 Kings	3 Kingdoms (comprising 1 Kings)	Additions to Esther
2 Kings	4 Kingdoms (comprising 2 Kings)	Prayer of Azariah and the Song of the Three Jews
1 Chronicles	1 Chronicles	Susanna
2 Chronicles	2 Chronicles	Bel and the Dragon
Ezra	1 Esdras	1 Esdras
Nehemiah	2 Esdras	Psalm 151
Esther (includes six additions)	Nehemiah	2 Esdras
Job	Tobit	Letter of Jeremiah
Psalms	Judith	
Proverbs	Esther (includes six additions)	
Ecclesiastes	1 Maccabees	
Song of Songs	2 Maccabees	
Isaiah	3 Maccabees	
Jeremiah	Psalms (includes Psalm 151)	
Lamentations	Job	
Ezekiel	Proverbs	
Daniel (includes three additions)	Ecclesiastes	
Hosea	Song of Songs	
Joel	Wisdom of Solomon	
Amos	Ecclesiasticus or the Wisdom of Jesus Son of Sirach	
Obadiah	Hosea	
Jonah	Amos	
Micah	Micah	
Nahum	Joel	
Habakkuk	Obadiah	
Zephaniah	Jonah	
Haggai	Nahum	
Zechariah	Habakkuk	
Malachi	Zephaniah	
1 Maccabees	Haggai	
2 Maccabees	Zechariah	
Judith	Malachi	
Tobit	Isaiah	
Ecclesiasticus or the Wisdom of Jesus Son of Sirach	Jeremiah	
Wisdom of Solomon	Baruch with the Letter of Jeremiah	
Baruch with the Letter of Jeremiah	Lamentations of Jeremiah	
	Epistle of Jeremiah	
	Ezekiel	
	Daniel (includes three additions)	
	4 Maccabees (this book is included in an appendix)	
	Prayer of Manasseh (this book is included in an appendix)	

Appendix 4: The Old Testament and the Early Church Fathers

Books in Question: Final Books in Protestant Old Testament	Eastern Church Fathers								Western Church Fathers			
	Melito of Sardis (ca. 180)	Origen (ca. 185 - 254)	Athanasius (ca. 367)	Synopsis Scripturae Sacrae (350-370)	Cyril of Jerusalem (ca. 350)	Gregory of Nazianzus (ca. 370)	Bryennios Canon (mid 4th century)	Epiphanius (ca. 315-403)	Hilary of Poitiers (ca. 315-367)	Jerome (ca. 342-420)	Augustine (ca. 354-430)	Rufinus (ca. 345-410)
Genesis	x	x	x	x	x	x	x	x	x	x	x	x
Exodus	x	x	x	x	x	x	x	x	x	x	x	x
Leviticus	x		x	x	x	x	x	x		x	x	x
Numbers	x		x	x	x	x	x	x		x	x	x
Deuteronomy	x	x	x	x	x	x	x	x	x	x	x	x
Joshua	x	x	x	x	x	x	x	x	x	x	x	x
Judges	x	x	x	x	x	x	x	x	x	x	x	x
Ruth	x	x	x	x	x	x	x	x	x	x	x	x
1 Samuel	x	x	x	x	x	x	x	x	x	x	x	x
2 Samuel	x	x	x	x	x	x	x	x	x	x	x	x
1 Kings	x	x	x	x	x	x	x	x	x	x	x	x
2 Kings	x	x	x	x	x	x	x	x	x	x	x	x
1 Chronicles	x	x	x	x	x	x	x	x	x	x	x	x
2 Chronicles	x	x	x	x	x	x	x	x	x	x	x	x
Ezra	x	x	x	x	x	x		x	x	x	x	x
Nehemiah		x	x	x	x	x		x	x	x	x	x
Esther		x	x		x		x	x	x	x	x	x
Job	x	x	x	x	x	x	x	x	x	x	x	x
Psalms	x	x	x	x	x	x	x	x	x	x	x	x
Proverbs	x	x	x	x	x	x	x	x	x	x	x	x
Ecclesiastes	x	x	x	x	x	x	x	x	x	x	x	x
Song of Songs	x	x	x	x	x	x	x	x	x	x	x	x
Isaiah	x	x	x	x	x	x	x	x	x	x	x	x
Jeremiah	x	x	x	x	x	x	x	x	x	x	x	x
Lamentations	x	x	x	x	x	x		x	x	x	x	x
Ezekiel	x	x	x	x	x	x	x	x	x	x	x	x
Daniel	x	x	x	x	x	x	x	x	x	x	x	x
Hosea	x	x	x	x	x	x	x	x	x	x	x	x
Joel	x	x	x	x	x	x	x	x	x	x	x	x
Amos	x	x	x	x	x	x	x	x	x	x	x	x
Obadiah	x	x	x	x	x	x	x	x	x	x	x	x
Jonah	x	x	x	x	x	x	x	x	x	x	x	x
Micah	x	x	x	x	x	x	x	x	x	x	x	x
Nahum	x	x	x	x	x	x	x	x	x	x	x	x
Habakkuk	x	x	x	x	x	x	x	x	x	x	x	x
Zephaniah	x	x	x	x	x	x	x	x	x	x	x	x
Haggai	x	x	x	x	x	x	x	x	x	x	x	x
Zechariah	x	x	x	x	x	x	x	x	x	x	x	x
Malachi	x	x	x	x	x	x	x	x	x	x	x	x

APPENDIX 4: OLD TESTAMENT AND EARLY CHURCH FATHERS

Books in Question: Apocrypha	Eastern Church Fathers								Western Church Fathers			
	Melito of Sardis (ca. 180)	Origen (ca. 185-254)	Athanasius (ca. 367)	Synopsis Scripturae Sacrae (350-370)	Cyril of Jerusalem (ca. 350)	Gregory of Nazianzus (ca. 370)	Bryennios Canon (mid 4th century)	Epiphanius (ca. 315-403)	Hilary of Poitiers (ca. 315-367)	Jerome (ca. 342-420)	Augustine (ca. 354-430)	Rufinus (ca. 345-410)
1 Esdras								x				
2 Esdras				x				x				
Tobit		x							x		x	x
Judith		x							x		x	x
Six Additions to Esther		x									x	
1 Maccabees		x									x	x
2 Maccabees		x									x	x
3 Maccabees												
Psalm 151												
Ecclesiasticus or the Wisdom of Jesus Son of Sirach		x									x	x
Baruch			x		x						x	
Prayer of Azariah and the Song of the Three Jews											x	
Susanna		x									x	
Bel and the Dragon											x	
4 Maccabees												
Prayer of Manasseh												
Wisdom of Solomon	x	x									x	x
Epistle of Jeremiah		x	x		x				x		x	

Shaded rows denote unanimous agreement on those texts considered authoritative.

Source: L. M. McDonald, The Biblical Canon: Its Origin, Transmission, and Authority (Grand Rapids, MI: Baker Academic, 2006), 180–184.

Appendix 5: Apostolic Fathers and the Texts They Valued

	Apostolic Fathers and the Texts They Valued	
Date	**Author**	**Material**
AD 96	Clement of Rome – Bishop of Rome[1]	First Epistle of Clement – Cites mostly the Old Testament Scriptures but shows an awareness of the gospel of Matthew and several other eventual New Testament writings, especially Paul's letters.[2]
AD 96 to 100[3]	Unknown[4]	Epistle of Barnabas – This pseudonymous letter reflects much of the material found in the New Testament. In particular, the role and person of Jesus is explained in a manner that parallels the writers of the New Testament gospels and Epistles.[5]
AD 100 to 120s	Papias – Bishop of Hierapolis in Asia Minor[6]	Reasonable evidence suggests that Papias knew about the gospels of Matthew and Mark in AD 100 and Luke and John by the 120s, based on citations of Papias in other historical writings.[7]
AD 110	Ignatius – Bishop of Antioch[8]	The letters of Ignatius show an awareness of the gospels of Matthew and John,[9] and they include references and allusions to most of Paul's letters.[10]
AD 110[11]	Polycarp – Bishop of Smyrna[12]	Letter to the Philippians – It is probable in this letter that Polycarp reflects knowledge of the gospels of Matthew and Luke. He also includes probable references to the New Testament writings of 1 Peter, 1 or 2 John, and Ephesians.[13]
AD 124 to 132[14]	Aristides – Apologist of Athens[15]	In the Apology of Aristides written to Emperor Hadrian, there are good indicators of his knowledge of all four gospel writings, which he recommends that the emperor reads.[16]

APPENDIX 5: APOSTOLIC FATHERS AND THE TEXTS THEY VALUED

Apostolic Fathers and the Texts They Valued		
Date	Author	Material
AD 130 to 140[17]	Unknown[18]	2 Clement – A pseudo-Clementine letter that shows varying degrees of dependence on the synoptic gospels of Matthew, Mark, and Luke.[19]
AD 140[20]	Unknown[21]	Apocryphon of James – A Gnostic work that was written in opposition to the four gospels and, therefore, acknowledges their existence and prevalence.[22]
AD 140s	Unknown[23]	Epistle of the Apostles – Possibly written in response to the Gnostic work above, this text purports to be a letter written by all of the apostles to reaffirm orthodox teaching. It alludes to all four Gospels with a heavy emphasis on John, Matthew, and Luke.[24]
AD 155 to 160[25]	Justin Martyr – Apologist/Philosopher based in Rome[26]	Dialogue with Trypho – The author refers to the "Memoir of the Apostles," and there are strong indicators that this is another form of the synoptic gospels of Matthew, Mark, and Luke.[27]
AD 160[28]	Ptolemy – Gnostic teacher[29]	Letter to Flora – The author cites the gospel of John, Ephesians, and Romans in this letter that seeks to define the integrity of the Jewish Scriptures.[30]
AD 160 to 170[31]	Tatian – Apologist (student of Justin)[32]	Diatessaron – The first harmonization of the four gospels combined with other gospel traditions.[33] Diatessaron means "through the four."[34]
AD 175 to 177[35]	Unknown[36]	Martyrs of Lyons and Vienne – This letter, which was preserved in Eusebius's Ecclesiastical History, contains many references, allusions, and quotations from New Testament literature.[37]
AD 170 to 180s[38]	Theophilus – Bishop of Antioch	Gospel Harmony – Harmonization of the four gospels[39] in a similar form to the Diatessaron.

Apostolic Fathers and the Texts They Valued		
Date	**Author**	**Material**
AD 190 to 200[40]	Theophilus – Bishop of Antioch[41]	To Autolycus – An apologetic work that intended to answer charges made against Christians in order to win over skeptics.[42] He utilizes the gospels of Matthew, Luke, and John to make his case.[43]
AD 180[44]	Irenaeus – Bishop of Lyon[45]	Against Heresies – Irenaeus argues for the exclusivity of the four gospels and alludes to other New Testament texts in this work.[46]
AD 180 to 215[47]	Clement – Theologian in Alexandria[48]	In all of his extant works, Clement makes 1,672 references to the four gospels.[49]
Circa AD 150[50]	Marcion – Theologian in Rome[51]	Antitheses[52] – Produced a list of books to be read in his churches that included the gospel of Luke and ten letters of Paul[53] (Galatians, 1 and 2 Corinthians, Romans, 1 and 2 Thessalonians, Ephesians, Colossians, Philippians, and Philemon).[54]
Circa AD 190[55]	Melito – Bishop of Sardis[56]	Wrote a commentary on the book of Revelation.[57]
AD 207 to 212[58]	Tertullian – Theologian of Carthage[59]	The Five Books Against Marcion[60] – Tertullian acknowledges the four gospels in this work.[61]
AD 197 to 212[62]	Tertullian – Theologian of Carthage[63]	Prescription Against Heretics – Refers to thirteen letters of Paul, Acts, 1 John, 1 Peter, Jude, and Revelation.

Appendix 6: Gnostic Gospels

Material	Estimated Date of Authorship	Description
Infancy Gospel of Thomas	Somewhere between 1st and 6th century[1]	A collection of stories centered upon Jesus's childhood and his miracle-working abilities. Many of the accounts do not portray Jesus in a favorable light; for example, he uses his supernatural powers to kill off playmates who irritate him and humiliates teachers who discipline him.[2]
The Proto-Gospel of James	Late 2nd century[3]	An account of the events leading up to and immediately following the birth of Jesus with the primary focus being on Jesus's mother Mary's upbringing, young life, and engagement to Joseph.[4]
The Gospel of Pseudo-Matthew	Mid 7th century[5]	A Latin reworking of the Proto-Gospel of James, which has removed some stories and replaced them with a narrative regarding the holy family's flight to Egypt. On this journey, the infant Jesus performs numerous miracles including the taming of dragons, making a palm tree bend down to deliver fruit to a famished Mary, and the bowing down of Egyptian pagan temple idols to worship him.[6]
The Latin Infancy Gospels (J Composition) Arundel Form	Mid 7th century to 8th century[7]	A reworking of the Proto-Gospel of James and of the Gospel of Pseudo-Matthew. Additional unique material included are accounts of the conversations of Joseph and his son Symeon both before and after Jesus's birth, declarations made by the midwife and the wise men regarding Mary and Jesus, and a story of a compassionate robber.[8]
History of Joseph the Carpenter	Late 6th or early 7th century[9]	Outlines the central moments in Joseph's life including his background, relationship with Mary, role in the birth and fathering of Jesus, and death.[10]

Material	Estimated Date of Authorship	Description
The Gospel of the Nazarenes	Mid 2nd century[11]	Contains accounts of Jesus's baptism, teaching, healing, and death. The gospel enjoyed a long life with sources attesting to it from the late 2nd to 13th century.[12]
The Gospel of the Ebionites	Mid to late 2nd century[13]	A gospel account which conflates the gospels of Matthew, Mark, and Luke. It covers Jesus's baptism, his call of the twelve, his public ministry, the Last Supper, and his death.[14]
The Gospel according to the Hebrews	Early-mid 2nd century[15]	In a similar manner to the Gospel of the Nazarenes, this gospel is a narrative account of Jesus's entire public ministry, from beginning to end, and including his resurrection. This gospel was known and used in Egypt.[16]
The Gospel according to the Egyptians	Mid 2nd century[17]	This gospel cannot be found in any surviving manuscripts but only in the citations of the late 2nd century church father Clement of Alexandria. As such, it's difficult to say anything definitive about the extent and character of the writing, but the six quotations we have deal with matters of sexual abstinence, relation of the genders, and childbirth.[18]
A Gospel Harmony: The Diatessaron	AD 160 to 170[19]	The first harmonization of the four biblical gospels combined with other gospel traditions,[20] authored by the Christian philosopher and theologian Tatian.[21] Diatessaron means "through the four."[22]
Papyrus Berlin 11710	Unknown – Surviving manuscript is dated to the 6th century[23]	This surviving manuscript of two very small papyrus leaves records a brief conversation between Jesus and his disciple Nathaniel. The text seems to be modeled on John 1:49 and 29, and the fragments' diminutive size suggests that it may have formed part of an amulet, which is a small text used for the purposes of magic.[24]

APPENDIX 6: GNOSTIC GOSPELS 185

Material	Estimated Date of Authorship	Description
Papyrus Cairo 10735	Unknown – Surviving manuscript is dated to the 6th or 7th century[25]	Consists of one papyrus leaf, which provides an expanded version of the infancy narratives contained in Matthew and Luke. It's comprised of two parts, with the first referring to the holy family's flight to Egypt and the second relating to the work of John the Baptist.[26]
Papyrus Egerton 2 and Papyrus Koln 255	AD 150 to 200[27]	Consists of five fragmentary papyrus leaves (two of which are uninterpretable), which record four narrative accounts that have many similarities with the New Testament gospels. Of particular note is the recording of a miracle that Jesus performed by the Jordan River that is not mentioned in the other biblical gospels.[28]
Papyrus Merton 51	Unknown – Surviving text is dated to the 3rd century[29]	Consists of one papyrus leaf that may or may not indicate the existence of an unknown gospel. The small text recounts Jesus's discourse about good trees bearing good fruit and bad trees the opposite, somewhat paralleling similar passages in Luke and Mark.[30]
Papyrus Oxyrhynchus 210	Unknown – Surviving text is dated to the 3rd century[31]	Consists of two fragments, which make its reconstruction difficult. Similar to the fragment above, this fragment recounts Jesus's discourse pertaining to fruit.[32]
Papyrus Oxyrhynchus 840	2nd or 3rd century[33]	Consists of a single parchment leaf that was part of a larger text. The text we have recounts a confrontation between Jesus and a high priest reminiscent of the accounts in Mark 7:1-8 and Luke 11:37-41. The author records that the high priest is a Pharisee, demonstrating his or her ignorance of Jewish customs and potentially revealing Christian bias.[34]

Material	Estimated Date of Authorship	Description
Papyrus Oxyrhynchus 1224	Unknown – Surviving text is dated to the 4th century[35]	Comprises several papyrus fragments of a larger unknown corpus. The fragments that are readable convey four different passages relating to the following topics: • A firsthand account of a dream where the author speaks with Jesus • A questioning of Jesus in a hostile manner regarding his "new teaching" • A controversy regarding Jesus's interactions with sinners • An urging from Jesus to pray for one's enemies[36]
Papyrus Oxyrhynchus 2949	Unknown[37]	Consisting of two small papyrus fragments with thirteen lines of text. This piece tells of someone called Joseph, the friend of Pilate, requesting Jesus's body for burial. Pilate then asks Herod to return the body, and that is the extent of the text.[38]
Papyrus Oxyrhynchus 4009	Unknown – Surviving text is dated to the 2nd or 3rd century[39]	A single leaf of papyrus that recounts a short conversation between Peter and Jesus involving the treatment of Christ's followers (lambs) by those who would do them harm (wolves). The passage echoes themes found in the biblical gospel accounts of Matthew and Luke.[40]
Papyrus Vindobonensis G 2325 (The Fayum Fragment)	Unknown – Surviving text is dated to the 3rd century[41]	A single fragment, which was part of a much larger manuscript that has been lost. It contains Jesus's prediction of his disciples' flight and Peter's eventual denial of association with him as recorded in the biblical gospels of Mark and Matthew.[42]
The Gospel according to Thomas	AD 100 to 150[43]	This gospel is the most widely known, most studied, and most controversial of all the supposed gospels outside the New Testament. A fully copy of the gospel in Coptic was discovered in the Nag Hammadi library in 1945. Comprised entirely of sayings attributed to Jesus, there is no mention of his supposed miracles, death, or resurrection.[44]

APPENDIX 6: GNOSTIC GOSPELS

Material	Estimated Date of Authorship	Description
Agrapha	Various	A collection of the sayings of Jesus that have been recorded in other sources outside of the New Testament gospels and other gospels.[45]
The Gospel of Peter	Early to mid 2nd century[46]	A gospel that provides an alternative version of the death and resurrection of Jesus. The writing is similar in many respects to the biblical gospels, but its most striking difference pertains to its account of Jesus exiting the tomb. He emerges as tall as a mountain, with the cross trailing behind him and Jesus declaring that the message of salvation has been proclaimed in the realm of the dead.[47]
The Gospel of Judas	AD 140 to 150[48]	This gospel contains a series of dialogues between Jesus and his disciples during Passover week prior to his crucifixion. In these conversations, Jesus reveals the hidden truths of salvation to his disciples, especially Judas. There is no mention of his supposed death and resurrection.[49]
The Gospel of Philip	3rd century AD[50]	A collection of disparate Gnostic mystical reflections supposedly recorded by Jesus's disciple Philip. We have one manuscript of this gospel that was discovered at Nag Hammadi, and it possibly alludes to the nature of the relationship Jesus held with Mary Magdalene. However, due to the incomplete nature of the manuscript, we cannot determine what this supposed relationship was.[51]
Jesus's Correspondence with Abgar	Early 3rd century[52]	A supposed correspondence between Jesus and the Abgar, King of Edessa in eastern Syria who reigned from 4 BC to AD 7 and AD 13 to 50. The first letter written by Abgar requests that Jesus come to his homeland to heal him of his illness. In his reply, Jesus says he cannot come because he needs to fulfill his mission, but he will send an apostle to heal the king following his ascension.[53]

Material	Estimated Date of Authorship	Description
The Gospel of the Savior	End of the 2nd century[54]	An incomplete gospel that provides a somewhat stuttering account of events leading up to Jesus's death and a supposed resurrection appearance.[55]
The Discourse upon the Cross	At earliest, 8th century[56]	A discourse between Jesus and his disciples just prior to his ascension, where he discusses the meaning of the cross and the role it will play in the judgment of people. The narrative then moves retrospectively to the time just prior to the crucifixion and portrays Jesus singing a hymn of praise to the cross.[57]
The Gospel of Nicodemus (The Acts of Pilate) A	Mid 4th century[58]	A legendary gospel that deals exclusively with the happenings around Jesus's trial, death, and resurrection. It includes additional imaginative details to the traditional gospels, which may be attempting to achieve certain theological and ideological aims, such as establishing the divinity of Christ, the innocence of Pilate, and the hateful rejection of the Jewish people.[59]
The Gospel of Nicodemus (The Acts of Pilate) B	5th or 6th century[60]	A reworking of the text above that includes an entirely new narrative of eleven chapters detailing a "Descent into Hades." The narrative addresses the theological questions of why it was necessary for Jesus to become human and how he was able to overcome evil.[61]
The Report of Pontius Pilate (Anaphora Pilati)	4th or 5th century[62]	A report purported to have been written by Pontius Pilate to Emperor Tiberius outlining the events of Jesus's trial, death, and resurrection from the Roman governor's perspective. Potential motives of the account are to celebrate Jesus's miraculous character, to exonerate Pilate, and to incriminate the Jews.[63]

APPENDIX 6: GNOSTIC GOSPELS

Material	Estimated Date of Authorship	Description
The Handing Over of Pilate (Paradosis Pilati)	4th or 5th century[64]	A fictious account of the Roman governor being summoned to Rome and censured by Emperor Tiberius for his role in having Jesus crucified. Pilate repents of his deed, turns to Christ for salvation, and is beheaded.[65]
The Letter of Pilate to Claudius	Sometime between late 2nd century and 5th century[66]	A letter allegedly from Pilate written to Emperor Claudius. The themes in this letter resonate with those already raised above, namely that Pilate wasn't responsible for Jesus's death but rather the Jews were.[67]
The Letter of Herod to Pilate	Unknown – Earliest attestation of the letter is 6th or 7th century[68]	A letter allegedly written by Herod Antipas (the ruler who beheaded John the Baptist as accounted in the gospels) to Pontius Pilate not long after the death of Jesus. The letter once again paints Pilate in a good light while casting disparagement on Herod and the Jewish people who are responsible for killing Jesus.[69]
The Letter of Pilate to Herod	3rd century[70]	A fictitious letter written from Pontius Pilate to Herod. The letter is principally concerned with showing how Pilate, his wife (Procla), and the soldier Longinus (responsible for stabbing Jesus with a spear on the cross) all converted to become followers of Christ following Jesus's resurrection.[71]
The Letter of Tiberius to Pilate	11th century at the earliest[72]	A letter allegedly written by Emperor Tiberius to Pontius Pilate where he lashes out at Pilate for his wicked act of killing Jesus. The text then outlines the judicial sentence to be applied to Pilate, his accomplices, and the Jewish people. The letter then turns to an account which details the grisly execution of the sentences on all concerned.[73]

Material	Estimated Date of Authorship	Description
The Vengeance of the Savior (Vindicta Salvatoris)	8th century[74]	A narrative that outlines Pilate's imprisonment and condemnation but is primarily focused on the fate of the Jewish people. They are condemned for their role in the death of Jesus and are subsequently inflicted with horrible punishments, including the violent destruction of Jerusalem by the Roman rulers Titus and Vespasian.[75]
The Death of Pilate Who Condemned Jesus (Mors Pilati)	11th to 12th century[76]	This is an intriguing account of Pilate's ignominious fate after he had Jesus killed. The ailing Emperor Tiberius learns that Jesus is capable of healing him but discovers that Pilate has already had him executed. The emperor is eventually cured by the supernatural image of Jesus's face on the cloth of Veronica. However, he is still incensed over Pilate's unjust action and orders him to be imprisoned and executed, which ultimately ends in Pilate committing suicide in prison.[77]
The Narrative of Joseph of Arimathea	4th century at the earliest[78]	This is an alternative version of the biblical gospel death narrative told by Joseph of Arimathea, which emphasizes the betrayal of Judas and the events that transpired both at the crucifixion and after the resurrection. Legendary in nature, the text sometimes supplements and sometimes contradicts the biblical gospels on which it is partially based.[79]
The Gospel according to Mary	2nd century[80]	There is no complete copy of this gospel, but the fragments we currently have comprise half of the original text at most. It has Mary Magdalene recounting to the disciples teachings that Jesus had given her. The disciples Andrew and Peter respond to her in a highly skeptical manner as her teachings are at odds with their understanding of Jesus. The story ends with Levi defending Mary and instructing the disciples to continue proclaiming the gospel.[81]

ENDNOTES

PREFACE

1. C. S. Lewis, *God in the Dock: Essays on Theology and Ethics* (Grand Rapids, MI: Eerdmans, 1970), 101.

CHAPTER 1

1. T. D. Alexander, *Dictionary of the Old Testament - Pentateuch: A Compendium of Contemporary Biblical Scholarship* (Westmont, IL: InterVarsity Press, 2002), 161.
2. D. Alexander, *Creation or Evolution: Do We Have to Choose?* (Oxford, UK: Lion Hudson Plc), 192.
3. Alexander, *Creation or Evolution*, 193.
4. F. W. Bush, D. A. Hubbard, and W. S. Lasor, *Old Testament Survey* (Grand Rapids, MI: Eerdmans, 1996), 20.

CHAPTER 2

1. "Boxing Day Tsunami: How the Disaster Unfolded 10 Years Ago," ABC News, December 23, 2014, http://www.abc.net.au/news/2014-12-24/boxing-day-tsunami-how-the-disaster-unfolded/5977568.
2. "Mad Dog: Gaddafi's Secret World," BBC Channel 4, February 3, 2014, directed by Christopher Olgiati.
3. "Stephen Fry on God" |The Meaning of Life | RTÉ One," RTÉ – IRELAND'S NATIONAL PUBLIC SERVICE MEDIA, February 1, 2015, https://www.youtube.com/watch?v=-suvkwNYSQo.

CHAPTER 3

1. Amy Orr-Ewing, "Why Trust the Bible?" (lecture, RZIM Academy, accessed September 18, 2018).
2. Timothy P. Mahoney, *Patterns of Evidence: The Exodus* (Minneapolis, MN: Thinking Man Media, 2015), location 21 percent, Kindle.
3. Mahoney, *Patterns of Evidence*, location 37 percent, Kindle.
4. Robert Schiestl, "The Statue of an Asiatic Man from Tell El-Dab'a, Egypt," *Egypt and the Levant*, vol. 16 (2006): 173–185, www.jstor.org/stable/23790282.

5   M. Bietak, Avaris: *The Capital of the Hyksos; Recent Excavations at Tell el Dab'a* (London: British Museum Press, 1996), 5, 10, 20-23, 102.

6   Mahoney, *Patterns of Evidence*, location 22 percent, Kindle.

7   B. G. Wood, "Did the Israelites Conquer Jericho? A New Look at the Archaeological Evidence," *Biblical Archaeology Review* 16.2 (March/April 1990). January 19, 2024, https://library.biblicalarchaeology.org/article/did-the-israelites-conquer-jericho-a-new-look-at-the-archaeological-evidence

8   J. P. Free, *Archaeology and Bible History*, rev. and exp. by Howard F. Vos (Grand Rapids, MI: Zondervan Publishing House, 1992), 111.

9   The British Museum, *Room 9: Assyria: Nineveh*, track 7 on *Galleries of the British Museum*, https://music.apple.com/gb/album/room-9-assyria-nineveh/1471813599?i=1471813750; The British Museum, BBC, "Episode 21 – Lachish Reliefs," in *A History of the World*, http://www.bbc.co.uk/ahistoryoftheworld/about/transcripts/episode21/.

10 The British Museum, *Room 10b: Assyria: Siege of Lachish*, track 9 on *Galleries of the British Museum*, https://music.apple.com/gb/album/room-10b-assyria-siege-of-lachish/1471813599?i=1471813752.

11 2 Kings 18:13; 2 Chronicles 32:9.

12 The British Museum, *Room 10b: Assyria: Siege of Lachish*.

13 2 Kings 9:3–6.

14 Randall Price, *Zondervan Handbook of Biblical Archaeology* (Grand Rapids, MI: Zondervan Academic, 2017), 135.

15 *Object: The Black Obelisk*, The British Museum, https://www.britishmuseum.org/collection/object/W_1848-1104-1.

16 L. E. Pearce, "How Bad Was the Babylonian Exile?," *Biblical Archaeology Review* 42:5 (September/October 2016): https://members.bib-arch.org/Biblical-archaeology-review/42/5/7.

17 Daniel 6:1–28; 3:1–30.

18 *Clay Tablet; New Babylonian. Chronicle for Years 605-594 BC*, The British Museum, http://www.britishmuseum.org/research/collection_online/collection_object_details.aspx?objectId=320055&partId=1.

19 E. H. Cline, *Biblical Archaeology: A Very Short Introduction* (Oxford: Oxford University Press, 2009), 70.

20 Cline, *Biblical Archaeology*, 70.

21 Price, *Zondervan Handbook of Biblical Archaeology*, 139.

ENDNOTES

22 Pearce, "How Bad Was the Babylonian Exile?"

23 *Encyclopedia Britannica Online*, s.v. "Cyrus the Great," accessed July 1, 2020, https://www.britannica.com/biography/Cyrus-the-Great.

24 2 Chronicles 36:22–23; Ezra 1:2–4; 6:2–5.

25 *Object: The Cyrus Cylinder*, The British Museum, https://www.britishmuseum.org/collection/object/W_1880-0617-1941.

26 K. Kitchen, *On the Reliability of the Old Testament* (Grand Rapids, MI: W.B. Eerdmans, 2006), 7–64.

27 Price, *Zondervan Handbook of Biblical Archaeology*, 292–293.

28 Matthew 26:57–68.

29 Matthew 27:26; Mark 15:15; Luke 23:24; John 19:16.

30 Price, *Zondervan Handbook of Biblical Archaeology*, 274–275.

31 John 9:1–11.

32 Biblical Archaeology Society Staff, "The Siloam Pool: Where Jesus Healed the Blind Man," Biblical Archaeology Society, February 21, 2023, https://www.biblicalarchaeology.org/daily/biblical-sites-places/biblical-archaeology-sites/the-siloam-pool-where-jesus-healed-the-blind-man.

33 Lawrence Mykytiuk, "53 People in the Bible Confirmed Archaeologically," Biblical Archaeology Society, September 13, 2022, https://www.biblicalarchaeology.org/daily/people-cultures-in-the-bible/people-in-the-bible/50-people-in-the-bible-confirmed-archaeologically/#note18r.

34 "Purdue Researcher Verifies the Existence of 53 People Mentioned in Hebrew Bible," Purdue University, June 6, 2017, https://www.purdue.edu/newsroom/releases/2017/Q2/purdue-researcher-verifies-the-existence-of-53-people-mentioned-in-hebrew-bible.html.

35 Price, *Zondervan Handbook of Biblical Archaeology*, 22.

36 Orr-Ewing, "Why Trust the Bible?"

37 J. McDowell, *Evidence That Demands a Verdict* (Milton Keynes, UK: Authentic Media, 2017), 102.

38 P. W. Flint, *The Dead Sea Scrolls* (Nashville: Abingdon Press, 2013), 103.

39 *Encyclopedia Britannica Online*, s.v. "History of Publishing," accessed July 14, 2020, https://www.britannica.com/topic/publishing/Books-in-the-early-Christian-era#ref397963.

40 C. L. Blomberg, *Can We Still Believe the Bible?* (Ada, MI; Brazos Press, 2014), 28.

41 Blomberg, *Can We Still Believe the Bible?*, 28–29.

42 M. D. Coogan, *The Oxford Encyclopedia of the Books of the Bible* (Oxford: Oxford University Press, 2011), 173–174.

43 Coogan, *The Oxford Encyclopedia of the Books of the Bible*, 176.

44 Blomberg, *Can We Still Believe the Bible?*, 29.

45 A. Anderson, W. Widder, and D. Mangum, *Textual Criticism of the Bible: Revised Edition*, Lexham Methods Series (Bellingham, WA: Lexham Press, 2018), 154.

46 Blomberg, *Can We Still Believe the Bible?*, 29.

47 "Is the Old Testament Fiction?," July 11, 2018, in *RZIM: Ask Away Broadcasts*, iTunes.

48 Blomberg, *Can We Still Believe the Bible?*, 16–17.

49 E. Hixson and P.J. Gurry, *Myths and Mistakes In New Testament Textual Criticism*, (Downers Grove, Illinois: IVP Academic), 69.

50 M. S. Silk, Homer: The Iliad (Cambridge: Cambridge University Press, 2004), 4.

51 *The Oxford History of the Classical World* (Oxford: Oxford University Press, 1986), 644.

52 Graham Speake, ed., *A Dictionary of Ancient History* (Blackwell Reference, 1994), 374.

53 R. Rutherford, *Classical Literature*: A Concise History (Blackwell Reference, 2005), 308.

54 *The Oxford History of the Classical World*, 853.

55 M. Schofield, "Authenticity and Chronology In: Plato (427–347 BC)," in *Routledge Encyclopedia of Philosophy* (London and New York: Routledge, 1998). Chronology regarding Plato's writings is difficult to establish, thus his years lived are presented as his potential authorship range.

56 Rutherford, *Classical Literature*, 307.

57 Speake, *A Dictionary of Ancient History*, 505.

58 *The Oxford History of the Classical World*, 837, 839.

59 Rutherford, *Classical Literature*, 307.

60 *The Oxford History of the Classical World*, 857.

ENDNOTES

61 B. D. Ehrman, *The Bible: An Historical and Literary Introduction* (Oxford: Oxford University Press, 2014), 385.

62 Blomberg, *Can We Still Believe the Bible?*, 17–28.

63 "Ehrman vs Wallace - Can We Trust the Text of the NT?," Bart D. Ehrman, February 3, 2020, https://www.youtube.com/watch?v=WRHjZCKRIu4&t=3586s.

64 *Encyclopedia Britannica Online*, s.v. "Suetonius," accessed December 14, 2021, https://www.britannica.com/biography/Suetonius.

65 Suetonius and T. Barton, *Lives of the Twelve Caesars* (Ware, Herfordshire: Wordsworth Editions Ltd., 1997), 8–9.

66 *The Oxford History of the Classical World*, 188.

67 *Encyclopedia Britannica Online*, s.v. "Herodotus."

68 Speake, *A Dictionary of Ancient History*, 614.

69 Speake, *A Dictionary of Ancient History*, 374.

70 J. B. Green, *Dictionary of Jesus and the Gospels* (Downers Grove, IL: InterVarsity Press, 2012), 576.

71 Green, *Dictionary of Jesus and the Gospels*, 561.

72 P. Nolland, *Luke 1-9:20* (Dallas, TX: Word Books, 1989), 59.

73 Green, *Dictionary of Jesus and the Gospels*, 422.

74 Silk, *Homer: The Iliad*, 4.

75 *The Oxford History of the Classical World*, 830.

76 *The Oxford History of the Classical World*, 644.

77 Speake, *A Dictionary of Ancient History*, 374.

78 *The Oxford History of the Classical World*, 831.

79 *The Oxford History of the Classical World*, 850.

80 *The Oxford History of the Classical World*, 853.

81 *The Oxford History of the Classical World*, 853.

82 Rutherford, *Classical Literature*, 307.

83 Rutherford, *Classical Literature*, 307.

84 Rutherford, *Classical Literature*, 307.

85 *The Oxford History of the Classical World*, 835.

86 *The Oxford History of the Classical World*, 835.

87 *Encyclopedia Britannica Online*, s.v. "Herodotus," accessed December 14, 2021, https://www.britannica.com/biography/Herodotus-Greek-historian.

88 *The Oxford History of the Classical World*, 857.

89 *The Oxford History of the Classical World*, 646.

90 *The Oxford History of the Classical World*, 857.

91 *The Oxford History of the Classical World*, 646.

92 Rutherford, *Classical Literature*, 311.

93 *The Oxford History of the Classical World*, 664.

94 Rutherford, *Classical Literature*, 127.

95 D. Wardle, *Suetonius*, 1st ed. (Oxford: Oxford University Press, 2014), 6.

96 Rutherford, *Classical Literature*, 129.

97 Shaye J. D. Cohen, "History and Historiography in the *Against Apion* of Josephus," *History and Theory* 27, no. 4 (December 1988): 1–11. This work was completed in the last decade of the first century AD or the first decade of the second century AD.

98 Flavius Josephus, *Against Apion*, trans. and ed. J. Barclay, vol. 10 (Boston: Brill Academic Publishers, 2007), 28–32.

99 Josephus, *Against Apion*, 30.

100 M. Goodman, J. Barton, and J. Muddiman, eds., *The Apocrypha* (Oxford: Oxford University Press, 2012), 4.

101 D. A. Carson, *The Enduring Authority of the Christian Scriptures* (Grand Rapids, MI: Eerdmans, 2016), 260.

102 L. M. McDonald, *The Biblical Canon: Its Origin, Transmission, and Authority* (Grand Rapids, MI: Baker Academic, 2006), 135.

103 Blomberg, *Can We Still Believe the Bible?*, 47.

104 R. D. Nelson, *The Old Testament: Canon, History, and Literature* (Nashville: Abingdon Press, 2019), 31.

105 Nelson, *The Old Testament*, 31.

106 McDonald, *The Biblical Canon*, 116.

107 McDonald, *The Biblical Canon*, 117.

108 McDonald, *The Biblical Canon*, 118.

109 Nelson, *The Old Testament*, 31.

110 McDonald, *The Biblical Canon*, 118.

ENDNOTES

111 Timothy Michael Law, *When God Spoke Greek* (Oxford: Oxford University Press, 2013), 59.

112 Carson, *The Enduring Authority of the Christian Scriptures*, 270.

113 Law, *When God Spoke Greek*, 85.

114 McDonald, *The Biblical Canon*, 119.

115 Nelson, *The Old Testament*, 30–31.

116 Nelson, *The Old Testament*, 34.

117 Nelson, *The Old Testament*, 34.

118 Law, *When God Spoke Greek*, 159.

119 Nelson, *The Old Testament*, 35.

120 Carson, *The Enduring Authority of the Christian Scriptures*, 271.

121 Nelson, *The Old Testament*, 35.

122 John McManners, ed., *The Oxford Illustrated History of Christianity* (Oxford: Oxford University Press, 1990), 686.

123 Nick Needham, *2,000 Years of Christ's Power: Vol. 1: The Age of the Early Church Fathers* (Fearn, Ross-shire: Christian Focus Publications, 2016), 41–44.

124 McManners, *The Oxford Illustrated History of Christianity*, 686.

125 Needham, *2,000 Years of Christ's Power*, 44–45.

126 McManners, *The Oxford Illustrated History of Christianity*, 686.

127 Needham, *2,000 Years of Christ's Power*, 49.

128 McManners, *The Oxford Illustrated History of Christianity*, 686.

129 W. B. Shelton, *Quest for the Historical Apostles: Tracing Their Lives and Legacies* (Grand Rapids, MI: Baker Academic, 2018), 71.

130 Shelton, *Quest for the Historical Apostles*, 76.

131 Shelton, *Quest for the Historical Apostles*, 96.

132 Shelton, *Quest for the Historical Apostles*, 65.

133 Shelton, *Quest for the Historical Apostles*, 105.

134 McManners, *The Oxford Illustrated History of Christianity*, 686.

135 Shelton, *Quest for the Historical Apostles*, 116–119.

136 Shelton, *Quest for the Historical Apostles*, 130–131.

137 Shelton, *Quest for the Historical Apostles*, 142.

138 Shelton, *Quest for the Historical Apostles*, 150–153.

139 Shelton, *Quest for the Historical Apostles*, 163.

140 Shelton, *Quest for the Historical Apostles*, 170.

141 Shelton, *Quest for the Historical Apostles*, 180.

142 Shelton, *Quest for the Historical Apostles*, 188.

143 Shelton, *Quest for the Historical Apostles*, 197.

144 E. Eve, *Behind the Gospels: Understanding the Oral Tradition* (London: SPCK Publishing, 2013), 19.

145 J. B Green and L. M. McDonald, eds., *The World of the New Testament: Cultural, Social, and Historical Contexts* (Grand Rapids, MI: Baker Academic, 2013), 349.

146 N. Taylor, "Early Christian Expectations Concerning the Return of Jesus: From Imminent Parousia to the Millennium," *Journal of Theology for Southern Africa*, vol. 104 (1999): 32–43.

147 McDonald, *The Biblical Canon*, 215.

148 C. White, *The Emergence of Christianity* (Westport, CT: Greenwood Press, 2007), 12.

149 McDonald, *The Biblical Canon*, 241.

150 McDonald, *The Biblical Canon*, 250.

151 Needham, *2,000 Years of Christ's Power*, 13.

152 McDonald, *The Biblical Canon*, 252–259.

153 D. Brown, *The Da Vinci Code* (Robert Langdon) (London: Transworld), 231–234, Kindle.

154 Brown, *The Da Vinci Code*, 231.

155 B. D. Ehrman, *Truth and Fiction in the Da Vinci Code: A Historian Reveals What We Really Know about Jesus, Mary Magdalene, and Constantine* (Oxford: Oxford University Press, 2006), 33.

156 Ehrman, *Truth and Fiction in the Da Vinci Code*, 32.

157 Needham, *2,000 Years of Christ's Power*, 148.

158 Needham, *2,000 Years of Christ's Power*, 151.

159 Needham, *2,000 Years of Christ's Power*, 151.

160 Needham, *2,000 Years of Christ's Power*, 199–201.

161 Needham, *2,000 Years of Christ's Power*, 201–202.

162 Needham, *2,000 Years of Christ's Power*, 175.

163 Brown, *The Da Vinci Code*, 231–234.

164 Ehrman, *Truth and Fiction in the Da Vinci Code*, 115.

165 *The Greek Ecclesiastical Historians of the First Six Centuries of the Christian Era*, 6 vols. (London: Samuel Bagster & Sons, 1846), 203–204.

166 "Constantine the Great," October 5, 2017, in *In Our Time*, radio broadcast, https://www.bbc.co.uk/programmes/b096gjw0.

167 Ehrman, *Truth and Fiction in the Da Vinci Code*, 38.

168 McDonald, *The Biblical Canon*, 310–311.

169 W. R. F. Browning, *Dictionary of the Bible* (Oxford: Oxford University Press, 2009), 373.

170 Needham, *2,000 Years of Christ's Power*, 24.

171 Browning, *Dictionary of the Bible*, 373.

172 B. D. Ehrman, *The Other Gospels: Accounts of Jesus from Outside the New Testament* (Oxford: Oxford University Press, 2013), 5.

173 Ehrman, *The Other Gospels*, 6.

174 Ehrman, *The Other Gospels*, 19.

175 Ehrman, *The Other Gospels*, 18.

176 Ehrman, *The Other Gospels*, 104.

177 Ehrman, *The Other Gospels*, 104.

178 Ehrman, *The Other Gospels*, 109.

179 Ehrman, *The Other Gospels*, 109.

180 Ehrman, *The Other Gospels*, 113.

181 Ehrman, *The Other Gospels*, 112.

182 McDonald, *The Biblical Canon*, 235.

183 McDonald, *The Biblical Canon*, 235.

184 Ehrman, *The Other Gospels*, 120.

185 C. E. Hill, *Who Chose the Gospels? Probing the Great Gospel Conspiracy* (Oxford: Oxford University Press, 2010), 105.

186 Ehrman, *The Other Gospels*, 160.

187 Ehrman, *The Other Gospels*, 158.

188 Ehrman, *The Other Gospels*, 196.

189 Ehrman, *The Other Gospels*, 193.

190 Ehrman, *The Other Gospels*, 202.

191 Ehrman, *The Other Gospels*, 202.

192 B. D. Ehrman, *Lost Christianities: The Battle for Scripture and the Faiths We Never Knew* (Oxford: Oxford University Press, 2005), 11.

193 Ehrman, *Lost Christianities*, 122.

194 Ehrman, *Truth and Fiction in the Da Vinci Code*, 60, 63.

195 Brown, *The Da Vinci Code*, 246.

196 P. J. Williams, *Can We Trust the Gospels?* (Wheaton, IL: Crossway, 2018), 31–50.

197 "Peter J Williams & Bart Ehrman: The Story of Jesus: Are the Gospels Historically Reliable?," Premier Unbelievable?, October 25, 2019, 30:30–32:50, https://www.youtube.com/watch?v=ZuZPPGvF_2I&t=3419s.

198 C. S. Lewis, *God in the Dock: Essays on Theology and Ethics* (Grand Rapids, MI: Eerdmans, 1970), 101.

CHAPTER 4

1 John Dickson, *Is Jesus History?* (Charlotte, NC: The Good Book Company, 2019), 28–30, Kindle.

2 Dickson, *Is Jesus History?*, 76.

3 Dickson, *Is Jesus History?*, 76–78.

4 J. McDowell, *Evidence That Demands a Verdict* (Milton Keynes, UK: Authentic Media, 2017), 153.

5 Melvyn Bragg, "Josephus," May 21, 2015, in *In Our Time*, radio broadcast, http://www.bbc.co.uk/programmes/b05vfdzl.

6 McDowell, *Evidence That Demands a Verdict*, 153.

7 *Jewish Antiquities*, 18.63–64, emphasis added. Dickson, *Is Jesus History?*, 80.

8 Dickson, *Is Jesus History?*, 80.

9 *Jewish Antiquities*, 20.200. Dickson, *Is Jesus History?*, 83.

10 McDowell, *Evidence That Demands a Verdict*, 147–150.

11 S. Hornblower, A. Spawforth, and E. Eidinow, *The Oxford Classical Dictionary*, 4th ed. (Oxford: Oxford University Press, 2012), 782.

12 Hornblower, Spawforth, and Eidinow, *The Oxford Classical Dictionary*, 1420.

13 Hornblower, Spawforth, and Eidinow, *The Oxford Classical Dictionary*, 59.

14 Oxford Bibliographies, s.v. "Cleopatra," by Duane W. Roller, April 28, 2014, https://www.oxfordbibliographies.com/view/document/obo-9780195389661/obo-9780195389661-0130.xml.

15 "Norm Macdonald on the State of Comedy Today and 'Saturday Night Live' - #TBT," Larry King, May 22, 2013, https://www.youtube.com/watch?v=V-CSz_L1e9g.

16 John 8:1-11.

17 Matthew 23:1-39.

18 Matthew 5:44.

19 Luke 12:49-53.

20 M. Casey, *Jesus of Nazareth: An Independent Historian's Account of His Life and Teaching* (London: T&T Clark, 2010), 145.

21 M. A. Powell, *Jesus as a Figure in History: How Modern Historians View the Man from Galilee*, 2nd ed. (Louisville, KY: Westminster John Knox Press, 2013), 206.

22 For further reading, please see B. Witherington, "Biblical Views: The Turn of the Christian Era; The Tale of Dionysius Exiguus," *Biblical Archaeology Review* 43:6 (November/December 2017).

23 Matthew 2:13-18.

24 B. M. Metzger and M. D. Coogan, *The Oxford Companion to the Bible* (Oxford: Oxford University Press, 1993), 356.

25 H. K. Bond, *The Historical Jesus: A Guide for the Perplexed* (London: T&T Clark, 2012), 78-79.

26 Bond, *The Historical Jesus*, 79.

27 Bond, *The Historical Jesus*, 79-80.

28 Bond, *The Historical Jesus*, 80-81.

29 Bond, *The Historical Jesus*, 132-133.

30 Bond, *The Historical Jesus*, 82.

31 N. T. Wright, *Jesus and the Victory of God* (Minneapolis, MN: Fortress Press, 1996), 147.

32 Wright, *Jesus and the Victory of God*, 147.

33 J. Stott and A. McGrath, *The Cross of Christ with Study Guide*, 20th ed. (Downers Grove, IL: InterVarsity Press, 2021), 56.

34 Wright, *Jesus and the Victory of God*, 147–148.

CHAPTER 5

1 Bart Ehrman, *Truth and Fiction in the Da Vinci Code: A Historian Reveals What We Really Know about Jesus, Mary Magdalene, and Constantine* (New York: Oxford University Press, 2004), 115.

2 Craig Blomberg, Ph.D., being interviewed by Lee Strobel, explains why the game of telephone is not a good analogy for how oral traditions are passed on. As quoted by Lee Strobel in *The Case for Christ* (Grand Rapids, MI: Zondervan Publishing House, 1998), 56.

3 As quoted by Strobel in *The Case for Christ*, 56.

4 M. Hengel, *Crucifixion in the Ancient World* (London: SCM Press, 1977), 22–25.

5 Strobel, *The Case for Christ*, 212.

6 1 Corinthians 1:23.

CHAPTER 6

1 Genesis 12:1–3.

2 Abraham is the same person as Abram. The Bible recounts God changing his name in Genesis 17:5.

3 W. C. Kaiser Jr., "Jesus in the Old Testament," Gordon Conwell Theological Seminary, August 9, 2011, https://www.gordonconwell.edu/blog/jesus-in-the-old-testament

4 N. T. Wright, *Mark for Everyone*, New Testament for Everyone (Louisville, KY: Westminster John Knox Press, 2004), 1, Kindle.

5 R. J. Hutchinson, *Searching for Jesus: New Discoveries in the Quest for Jesus of Nazareth—and How They Confirm the Gospel Accounts* (Nashville: Nelson Books, 2015), 7.5 percent, E-edition.

6 Mark 6:5–6.

7 Mark 7:24–30.

8 Matthew 12:38–42; 16:1–4; Mark 8:11–13.

9 Mark 1:34; 5:43; 7:36; 8:30.

10 J. Dickson, *A Doubter's Guide to Jesus: An Introduction to the Man from Nazareth for Believers and Skeptics* (Grand Rapids, MI: Zondervan, 2018), 73–77.

11 K. Sawrey, *The Infographic Bible: Visualising the Drama of God's Word* (New York: HarperCollins, 2018), 149.

12 N. T. Wright, *Simply Jesus: Who He Was, What He Did, Why It Matters* (London: SPCK, 2006), 26–37.

13 N. T. Wright, *Simply Good News: Why the Gospel Is News And What Makes It Good* (London: SPCK, 2015), 29.

14 N. T. Wright, *How God Became King* (New York: Harper Collins, 2012), 64.09 percent, E-book edition.

15 Wright, *How God Became King*, 83.64 percent, E-book edition.

16 W. L. Craig, *Atonement and the Death of Christ: An Exegetical, Historical, and Philosophical Exploration* (Waco, TX: Baylor University Press, 2020), 18–19.

17 Craig, *Atonement and the Death of Christ*, 19.

18 R. C. Sproul, *The Holiness of God* (Carol Stream, IL: Tyndale House Publishers, 1998), 37, Kindle.

19 Craig, *Atonement and the Death of Christ*, 30.

20 Craig, *Atonement and the Death of Christ*, 21.

21 Craig, *Atonement and the Death of Christ*, 22.

22 C. S. Lewis, *Mere Christianity* (New York: Harper Collins, 1952), 33, Kindle.

23 J. Stott and A. McGrath, *The Cross of Christ with Study Guide*, 20th ed. (Downers Grove, IL: InterVarsity Press, 2021), 71.

24 Stott and McGrath, *The Cross of Christ with Study Guide*, 74.

25 S. Hornblower, A. Spawforth, E. Eidinow, *The Oxford Classical Dictionary*, 4th ed. (Oxford: Oxford University Press, 2012), 1491.

26 H. A. Rigg, "Thallus: The Samaritan?," *Harvard Theological Review* 34, no. 2 (1941): 111–119.

27 Hornblower, Spawforth, and Eidinow, *The Oxford Classical Dictionary*, 1172.

28 N. P. L. Allen, "Thallus and Phlegon: Solar Eclipse in Jerusalem c. 33 CE?" Akroterion 63 (2019): 7–8.

29 Allen, "Thallus and Phlegon," 5.

30 John Stott, *The Cross of Christ* (Downers Grove, IL: InterVarsity Press, 2006), 67.

31 Stott, *The Cross of Christ*, 108.

32 G. Lanier, "Curtain Torn in Two: What Did the Tearing of the Veil Accomplish?," The Gospel Coalition, April 2, 2021, https://www.thegospelcoalition.org/article/veil-torn-jesus-cross/.

CHAPTER 7

1 C. S. Lewis, *Mere Christianity* (New York: HarperCollins, 1952), 4, Kindle.

2 "The Argument from Morality – Debunked (William Lane Craig's Moral Argument Refuted)," Rationality Rules, March 5, 2017, https://www.youtube.com/watch?v=FQfujdlO4oY.

3 Richard Dawkins, *The God Delusion* (London: Black Swan, 2017), 220–221.

4 Dawkins, *The God Delusion*, 221.

5 Dawkins, *The God Delusion*, 31.

CHAPTER 8

1 Steven Pinker, *The Better Angels of Our Nature* (London: Penguin Books, 2011), https://www.goodreads.com/work/quotes/16029496-the-better-angels-of-our-nature-why-violence-has-declined, accessed 17 July 2023

2 *Oxford English Dictionary*, s.v. "genocide," accessed November 29, 2018, https://en.oxforddictionaries.com/definition/genocide.

3 Deuteronomy 12:31; Leviticus 20:1–5.

4 M. Volf, *Free of Charge: Giving and Forgiving in a Culture Stripped of Grace* (Grand Rapids, MI: Zondervan, 2015), 138–139.

CHAPTER 9

1 P. Williams, "Does the Bible Support Slavery?," Be Thinking, accessed May 8, 2020, https://www.bethinking.org/bible/does-the-bible-support-slavery.

2 Williams, "Does the Bible Support Slavery?"

3 "Brian Zahnd's False Gospel and Fake Jesus," Mike Winger, 15:15–17:00, https://www.youtube.com/watch?v=QUNdh1u6774.

4 D. C. Snell, "Slavery in the Ancient Near East," in *The Cambridge World History of Slavery*, ed. K. Bradley and P. Cartledge (Cambridge: Cambridge University Press, 2011), 4.

5 Roth, U. "Paul and Slavery: Economic Perspectives." In *Paul and Economics: A Handbook*, edited by Thomas R. Blanton IV and Raymond Pickett, 165–170. Minneapolis, MN: Fortress, 2017.

6 Blanton and Pickett, *Paul and Economics*, 165–166.

7 Blanton and Pickett, *Paul and Economics*, 167.

8 R. McLaughlin, *Confronting Christianity* (Wheaton, IL: Crossway, 2019), loc. 3700, Kindle.

9 Williams, "Does the Bible Support Slavery?"

10 McLaughlin, *Confronting Christianity*, loc. 3700.

11 "Does Bible Support Slavery? What about Same-Sex Marriage?," Resource 777, accessed May 8, 2020, https://www.youtube.com/watch?v=849UukKbA7Q.

CHAPTER 10

1 C. Smith, *God's Good Design* (Youngstown, OH: Matthias Media, 2012), loc. 2755, Kindle.

2 Carol Meyers, *Rediscovering Eve* (Oxford: Oxford University Press, 2012), 181, Kindle.

3 Carol Meyers, "Was Ancient Israel a Patriarchal Society?," *Journal of Biblical Literature* 133, no. 1 (2014): 20.

4 Meyers, "Was Ancient Israel a Patriarchal Society?," 20–21.

5 Meyers, "Was Ancient Israel a Patriarchal Society?," 21–22.

6 Judges 4:4–5.

7 1 Kings 15:13; Jeremiah 13:18; 29:2.

8 Exodus 15:2–21; 1 Samuel 18:6–7; 2 Samuel 19:35; Ecclesiastes 2:8; Jeremiah 31:4.

9 Exodus 38:8; 1 Samuel 2:22.

10 Ezekiel 8:16–17.

11 Isaiah 8:3; Joel 2:28.

12 Meyers, "Was Ancient Israel a Patriarchal Society?," 26–27.

13 Paul Copan, *Is God a Moral Monster?* (Ada, MI: Baker Publishing Group, 2011), 119, Kindle.

14 A. Moody, "Child Sacrifice – From Moriah to Peru," The Gospel

Coalition, May 16, 2018, https://au.thegospelcoalition.org/article/child-sacrifice-moriah-peru/.

15 Copan, *Is God a Moral Monster?*, 97.

16 H. M. Knapp, "Jephthah's Daughter in English Post-Reformation Exegesis," *The Westminster Theological Journal* 80, no. 2 (2018): 286.

17 P. Lockwood, "Jephthah's Daughter: Canny and Courageous to the End (Judges 11-12)," *Lutheran Theological Journal* 53, no. 2 (2019): 74.

18 Hebrews 11:32–34.

19 Isaiah 3:16–17; 13:9–16; Jeremiah 13:15–27.

20 L. Gatiss, and B. G. Green, eds., *1-2 Thessalonians, 1-2 Timothy, Titus, Philemon* (Westmont, IL: InterVarsity Press, 2019), 112.

21 T. Wright, *Paul for Everyone: The Pastoral Letters* (London: SPCK, 2003), 21.

22 N. T. Wright, *Paul for Everyone: The Prison Letters: Ephesians, Philippians, Colossians and Philemon*, The New Testament for Everyone (London: SPCK, 2004), 65–66, Kindle.

23 C. S. Keener, "'Man and Woman' in Hawthorne," in *Dictionary of Paul and His Letters*, ed. R. P. Martin and D. G. Reid (Downers Grove, IL: IVP, 1993), 587.

24 Keener, "'Man and Woman' in Hawthorne," 587–588.

25 A. T. Lincoln, *Word Biblical Commentary: 42: Ephesians* (Dallas: Word, 1990), 387.

26 H. Koester, "The Role of Women in the Christian Churches in Paul's Day," BibleTexts.com, September 13, 1997.

27 N. T. Wright, *Luke for Everyone* (London: SPCK, 2001), 88–89.

28 N. T. Wright, *Mark for Everyone*, The New Testament for Everyone (Louisville, KY: Westminster John Knox Press, 2004), 95, Kindle.

29 D. M. Rhoads, "Jesus and the Syrophoenician Woman in Mark: A Narrative-Critical Study," *Currents in Theology and Mission* 47, no. 4 (2020): 7.

CHAPTER 12

1 *Encyclopedia Britannica*, s.v. "Crusades," by Thomas F. Madden, Gary Dickson, and Marshall W. Baldwin, December 29, 2020, https://www.britannica.com/event/Crusades.

2   T. Block, *A Fatal Addiction: War in the Name of God* (New York: Algora Publishing, 2012), 77.

3   Natasha Moore, *For the Love of God: How the Church is Better and Worse than You Ever Imagined* (Raleigh, NC: Centre for Public Christianity, 2019), loc. 220–235, Kindle.

4   "Third Crusade," November 29, 2001, in *In Our Time*, radio broadcast, https://www.bbc.co.uk/sounds/play/p005471s.

5   Luke 6:27.

6   Nigel Biggar, *In Defence of War* (Oxford: Oxford University Press, 2013), 7, Kindle.

7   Moore, *For the Love of God*, loc. 2928, Kindle.

8   Moore, *For the Love of God*, loc. 301, Kindle.

9   *Encyclopedia Britannica*, s.v. "Spanish Inquisition," by Edward A. Ryan, July 2, 2020, https://www.britannica.com/topic/Spanish-Inquisition.

10 "The Spanish Inquisition," June 22, 2006, in *In Our Time*, radio broadcast, https://www.bbc.co.uk/sounds/play/p003c1bw.

11 Moore, *For the Love of God*, loc. 1812, Kindle.

CHAPTER 13

1   C. Hackett and D. McClendon, "Christians Remain World's Largest Religious Group, but They Are Declining in Europe," Pew Research Center, April 5, 2017, https://www.pewresearch.org/fact-tank/2017/04/05/christians-remain-worlds-largest-religious-group-but-they-are-declining-in-europe/.

2   J. Renard, *The Handy Islam Answer Book* (Canton, MI: Visible Ink Press, 2015), 1–2.

3   L. E. Sullivan, *Religions of the World: An Introduction to Culture and Meaning* (Minneapolis, MN: Fortress Press, 2013), 274–276.

4   Renard, *The Handy Islam Answer Book*, 2.

5   W. Deming, *Understanding the Religions of the World: An Introduction* (Hoboken, NJ: John Wiley & Sons, 2015), 424–425.

6   Sullivan, *Religions of the World*, 62.

7   C. Partridge, *Introduction to World Religions* (Minneapolis, MN: Fortress Press, 2005), 134.

8   "Introduction to Hinduism: Religions," BBC, accessed December 4, 2019, https://www.bbc.co.uk/religion/religions/hinduism/ataglance/glance.shtml.

9   Sullivan, *Religions of the World*, 63-64.

10 Partridge, *Introduction to World Religions*, 157.

11 Partridge, *Introduction to World Religions*, 188-189.

12 Sullivan, *Religions of the World*, 80.

13 Partridge, *Introduction to World Religions*, 189.

14 Partridge, *Introduction to World Religions*, 188-202.

15 W. G. Oxtoby, R. C. Amore, A. Hussain, and A. F. Segal, *A Concise Introduction to World Religions*, 3rd ed. (Oxford: Oxford University Press, 2015), 390.

16 Partridge, *Introduction to World Religions*, 188-202.

17 J. L. Esposito, D. J. Fasching, and T. T. Lewis, *World Religions Today*, 5th ed. (Oxford: Oxford University Press, 2015), glossary.

CHAPTER 14

1   F. Chan, D. Yankoski, P. M. Sprinkle, and M. Beuving, *The Francis Chan Collection: Crazy Love, Forgotten God, Erasing Hell, and Multiply* (Colorado Springs: David C Cook, 2013), 58.

2   *The Devil's Advocate*, directed by Taylor Hackford, featuring K. Reeves, A. Pacino, and C. Theron (Burbank, CA, Warner Home Video, 1998).

3   C. S. Lewis, *The Great Divorce* (New York: HarperCollins Publishers, 1945), loc. 724, Kindle.

APPENDIX 2

1   M. Goodman, J. Barton, and J. Muddiman, eds., *The Apocrypha* (Oxford: Oxford University Press, 2012), 188.

2   Goodman, Barton, and Muddiman, *The Apocrypha*, 185.

3   Goodman, Barton, and Muddiman, *The Apocrypha*, 5.

4   J. McDowell, *Evidence That Demands a Verdict* (Milton Keynes, UK: Authentic Media, 2017), 38.

5   Goodman, Barton, and Muddiman, *The Apocrypha*, 218.

6   Goodman, Barton, and Muddiman, *The Apocrypha*, 14.

7   Goodman, Barton, and Muddiman, *The Apocrypha*, 14.

8   Goodman, Barton, and Muddiman, *The Apocrypha*, 21.
9   Goodman, Barton, and Muddiman, *The Apocrypha*, 21.
10 McDowell, *Evidence That Demands a Verdict*, 38.
11 Goodman, Barton, and Muddiman, *The Apocrypha*, 35.
12 Goodman, Barton, and Muddiman, *The Apocrypha*, 35.
13 Goodman, Barton, and Muddiman, *The Apocrypha*, 49.
14 R. D. Nelson, *The Old Testament: Canon, History, and Literature* (Nashville: Abingdon Press, 2019), 270.
15 D. A. deSilva, *Immersion Bible Studies: Apocrypha* (Nashville: Abingdon Press, 2013), 86.
16 Goodman, Barton, and Muddiman, *The Apocrypha*, 69.
17 Nelson, *The Old Testament*, 272.
18 Goodman, Barton, and Muddiman, *The Apocrypha*, 113.
19 Goodman, Barton, and Muddiman, *The Apocrypha*, 112.
20 Nelson, *The Old Testament*, 274.
21 Goodman, Barton, and Muddiman, *The Apocrypha*, 122.
22 Goodman, Barton, and Muddiman, *The Apocrypha*, 121.
23 Goodman, Barton, and Muddiman, *The Apocrypha*, 121–122.
24 Goodman, Barton, and Muddiman, *The Apocrypha*, 121.
25 Nelson, *The Old Testament*, 264.
26 Goodman, Barton, and Muddiman, *The Apocrypha*, 121–122.
27 Goodman, Barton, and Muddiman, *The Apocrypha*, 121, 124.
28 Goodman, Barton, and Muddiman, *The Apocrypha*, 121–122.
29 Goodman, Barton, and Muddiman, *The Apocrypha*, 212.
30 Goodman, Barton, and Muddiman, *The Apocrypha*, 129.
31 Nelson, *The Old Testament*, 276.
32 Goodman, Barton, and Muddiman, *The Apocrypha*, 5.
33 Nelson, *The Old Testament*, 279.
34 Goodman, Barton, and Muddiman, *The Apocrypha*, 216.
35 Nelson, *The Old Testament*, 283.
36 D. A. deSilva, *Introducing the Apocrypha: Message, Context, and Significance* (Grand Rapids, MI: Baker Academic, 2018), 321.

37 Nelson, *The Old Testament*, 283.

38 William P. Brown, *The Oxford Handbook of the Psalms*, Oxford Handbooks (New York: Oxford University Press, 2014), 5.

39 Brown, *The Oxford Handbook of the Psalms*, 175. Psalm 151 was first included in the Septuagint, and the Septuagint Psalter has been estimated to have been translated in the 2nd century BC. Most of the psalms were written from the second temple period (520 BC) onwards, thus the authorship of Psalm 151 could be between 520 and 100 BC.

40 Goodman, Barton, and Muddiman, *The Apocrypha*, 215.

APPENDIX 5

1 W. R. F. Browning, *Dictionary of the Bible* (Oxford: Oxford University Press, 2009), 64.

2 L. M. McDonald, *The Biblical Canon*: Its Origin, Transmission, and Authority (Grand Rapids, MI: Baker Academic, 2006), 220.

3 C. N. Jefford, *Reading the Apostolic Fathers: A Student's Introduction* (Ada, MI: Baker Publishing Group, 2012), 38.

4 McDonald, *The Biblical Canon*, 232.

5 Jefford, *Reading the Apostolic Fathers*, 48.

6 C. E. Hill, *Who Chose the Gospels? Probing the Great Gospel Conspiracy* (Oxford: Oxford University Press, 2010), 105.

7 Hill, *Who Chose the Gospels?*, 210–215.

8 Hill, *Who Chose the Gospels?*, 195.

9 Hill, *Who Chose the Gospels?*, 228.

10 Craig D. Allert, *A High View of Scripture? The Authority of the Bible and the Formation of the New Testament Canon* (Grand Rapids, MI: Baker Academic, 2007), 204.

11 Hill, *Who Chose the Gospels?*, 193.

12 Nick Needham, *2,000 Years of Christ's Power: Vol. 1: The Age of the Early Church Fathers* (Fearn, Ross-shire: Christian Focus Publications, 2016), 56.

13 Hill, *Who Chose the Gospels?*, 194.

14 Hill, *Who Chose the Gospels?*, 179.

15 Hill, *Who Chose the Gospels?*, 179.

16 Hill, *Who Chose the Gospels?*, 180–182.

17 McDonald, *The Biblical Canon*, 220.
18 McDonald, *The Biblical Canon*, 220.
19 McDonald, *The Biblical Canon*, 220.
20 Hill, *Who Chose the Gospels?*, 228.
21 Hill, *Who Chose the Gospels?*, 169.
22 Hill, *Who Chose the Gospels?*, 164–169.
23 Hill, *Who Chose the Gospels?*, 164–170.
24 Hill, *Who Chose the Gospels?*, 169–171.
25 Hill, *Who Chose the Gospels?*, 124.
26 Needham, *2,000 Years of Christ's Power*, 81–82.
27 Allert, *A High View of Scripture?*, 186.
28 McDonald, *The Biblical Canon*, 234.
29 McDonald, *The Biblical Canon*, 230.
30 McDonald, *The Biblical Canon*, 234–235.
31 McDonald, *The Biblical Canon*, 235.
32 Hill, *Who Chose the Gospels?*, 104.
33 McDonald, *The Biblical Canon*, 235.
34 Hill, *Who Chose the Gospels?*, 105.
35 McDonald, *The Biblical Canon*, 235.
36 McDonald, *The Biblical Canon*, 235.
37 McDonald, *The Biblical Canon*, 235.
38 Hill, *Who Chose the Gospels?*, 104.
39 Hill, *Who Chose the Gospels?*, 92–93.
40 McDonald, *The Biblical Canon*, 236.
41 Hill, *Who Chose the Gospels?*, 79.
42 Hill, *Who Chose the Gospels?*, 79.
43 Hill, *Who Chose the Gospels?*, 92.
44 Allert, *A High View of Scripture?*, 177.
45 Jefford, *Reading the Apostolic Fathers*, 250.
46 Allert, *A High View of Scripture?*, 192.

47 Jefford, *Reading the Apostolic Fathers*, 245. Clement lived from AD 160 to 215, and scholars have assumed that he didn't write before the age of 20.
48 Jefford, *Reading the Apostolic Fathers*, 245.
49 Hill, *Who Chose the Gospels?*, 72.
50 Allert, *A High View of Scripture?*, 204.
51 Jefford, *Reading the Apostolic Fathers*, 251.
52 Hill, *Who Chose the Gospels?*, 177.
53 McDonald, *The Biblical Canon*, 226.
54 Allert, *A High View of Scripture?*, 152.
55 Allert, *A High View of Scripture?*, 231.
56 Jefford, *Reading the Apostolic Fathers*, 252.
57 Allert, *A High View of Scripture?*, 231.
58 Hill, *Who Chose the Gospels?*, 44.
59 McDonald, *The Biblical Canon*, 254.
60 McDonald, *The Biblical Canon*, 271.
61 McDonald, *The Biblical Canon*, 254.
62 B. M. Litfin, *Getting to Know the Church Fathers: An Evangelical Introduction* (Grand Rapids, MI: Baker Academic, 2016), 86. We don't know a precise date, but this is the supposed span of his writing career.
63 McDonald, *The Biblical Canon*, 254.

APPENDIX 6

1 B. D. Ehrman, *The Other Gospels: Accounts of Jesus from Outside the New Testament* (Oxford: Oxford University Press, 2013), 5.
2 Ehrman, *The Other Gospels*, 6.
3 Ehrman, *The Other Gospels*, 19.
4 Ehrman, *The Other Gospels*, 18.
5 Ehrman, *The Other Gospels*, 39.
6 Ehrman, *The Other Gospels*, 38.
7 Ehrman, *The Other Gospels*, 59.
8 Ehrman, *The Other Gospels*, 58.
9 Ehrman, *The Other Gospels*, 79.

10 Ehrman, *The Other Gospels*, 78.

11 Ehrman, *The Other Gospels*, 104.

12 Ehrman, *The Other Gospels*, 104.

13 Ehrman, *The Other Gospels*, 109.

14 Ehrman, *The Other Gospels*, 109.

15 Ehrman, *The Other Gospels*, 113.

16 Ehrman, *The Other Gospels*, 112.

17 Ehrman, *The Other Gospels*, 117.

18 Ehrman, *The Other Gospels*, 116.

19 L. M. McDonald, *The Biblical Canon: Its Origin, Transmission, and Authority* (Grand Rapids, MI: Baker Academic, 2006), 235.

20 McDonald, *The Biblical Canon*, 235.

21 Ehrman, *The Other Gospels*, 120.

22 C. E. Hill, *Who Chose the Gospels? Probing the Great Gospel Conspiracy* (Oxford: Oxford University Press, 2010), 105.

23 Ehrman, *The Other Gospels*, 123.

24 Ehrman, *The Other Gospels*, 123.

25 Ehrman, *The Other Gospels*, 125.

26 Ehrman, *The Other Gospels*, 125.

27 Ehrman, *The Other Gospels*, 127–128.

28 Ehrman, *The Other Gospels*, 128.

29 Ehrman, *The Other Gospels*, 132.

30 Ehrman, *The Other Gospels*, 132.

31 Ehrman, *The Other Gospels*, 134.

32 Ehrman, *The Other Gospels*, 134.

33 Ehrman, *The Other Gospels*, 137.

34 Ehrman, *The Other Gospels*, 36.

35 Ehrman, *The Other Gospels*, 140.

36 Ehrman, *The Other Gospels*, 140.

37 Ehrman, *The Other Gospels*, 143.

38 Ehrman, *The Other Gospels*, 145.

39 Ehrman, *The Other Gospels*, 147.

40 Ehrman, *The Other Gospels*, 146.

41 Ehrman, *The Other Gospels*, 149.

42 Ehrman, *The Other Gospels*, 151.

43 Ehrman, *The Other Gospels*, 160.

44 Ehrman, *The Other Gospels*, 158.

45 Ehrman, *The Other Gospels*, 181.

46 Ehrman, *The Other Gospels*, 196.

47 Ehrman, *The Other Gospels*, 193.

48 Ehrman, *The Other Gospels*, 202.

49 Ehrman, *The Other Gospels*, 202.

50 B. D. Ehrman, *Lost Christianities: The Battle for Scripture and the Faiths We Never Knew* (New York: Oxford University Press, 2003), 11.

51 Ehrman, *Lost Christianities*, 122.

52 Ehrman, *The Other Gospels*, 215.

53 Ehrman, *The Other Gospels*, 214.

54 Ehrman, *The Other Gospels*, 218.

55 Ehrman, *The Other Gospels*, 219.

56 Ehrman, *The Other Gospels*, 227.

57 Ehrman, *The Other Gospels*, 227.

58 Ehrman, *The Other Gospels*, 233.

59 Ehrman, *The Other Gospels*, 234.

60 Ehrman, *The Other Gospels*, 255.

61 Ehrman, *The Other Gospels*, 255.

62 Ehrman, *The Other Gospels*, 268.

63 Ehrman, *The Other Gospels*, 267.

64 Ehrman, *The Other Gospels*, 273.

65 Ehrman, *The Other Gospels*, 72.

66 Ehrman, *The Other Gospels*, 277.

67 Ehrman, *The Other Gospels*, 276–277.

68 Ehrman, *The Other Gospels*, 280.

69 Ehrman, *The Other Gospels*, 280.
70 Ehrman, *The Other Gospels*, 283.
71 Ehrman, *The Other Gospels*, 283–284.
72 Ehrman, *The Other Gospels*, 286.
73 Ehrman, *The Other Gospels*, 285–288.
74 Ehrman, *The Other Gospels*, 290.
75 Ehrman, *The Other Gospels*, 289.
76 Ehrman, *The Other Gospels*, 301.
77 Ehrman, *The Other Gospels*, 300.
78 Ehrman, *The Other Gospels*, 306.
79 Ehrman, *The Other Gospels*, 305–306.
80 Ehrman, *The Other Gospels*, 315.
81 J. McDowell, *Evidence That Demands a Verdict* (Milton Keynes, UK: Authentic Media, 2017), 136.

LIST OF IMAGES AND ILLUSTRATIONS

Number	Description	Page
Figure 1	Behind the palace at Avaris — 12 special graves and memorial chapels built above them	13
Figure 2	Statue of Asiatic Man — Cairo Museum (The Basement)	14
Figure 3	Aerial view of Jericho, Tell es-Sultan, from the west	15
Figure 4	Lachish reliefs room — British Museum	17
Figure 5	Black Obelisk of Shalmaneser III, Side C, 858–824 BC — British Museum	17
Figure 6	Black Obelisk, Side A, Jehu of Israel bowing down — British Museum	17
Figure 7	Babylonian Chronicle, 605–594 BC, Jerusalem capture — British Museum	18
Figure 8	Jehoiachin Ration Tablet — Pergamon Museum	19
Figure 9	Cyrus Cylinder — British Museum	20
Figure 10	Ossuary of Joseph son of Caiaphas, from Jerusalem, 1st century AD — Israel Museum	22
Figure 11	Pontius Pilate limestone dedicatory inscription, 26–36 AD, from Caesarea — Israel Museum	23
Figure 12	Northern perimeter of the Pool of Siloam — Jerusalem	24
Figure 13	Rendering of the Pool of Siloam, Second Temple period	24
Figure 14	Distribution of New Testament manuscripts by century	31
Figure 15	Time distance of publication from the historical event	35

Figure 16	Paul's missionary journeys	47
Figure 17	Christian communities between AD 70 and 100	51
Figure 18	Model of the Jewish Temple: Second Temple period — Israel Museum	90
Figure 19	Layout of the Jewish Temple — Second Temple period	90
Figure 20	Statue of Judith	175

All images and illustrations have been used
with permission or licensed appropriately.

LIST OF TABLES

Number	Description	Page
Table 1	Manuscript Data from the Ancient World	29
Table 2	Time Gap from Estimated Date of Authorship to Earliest Manuscript	33
Table 3	Time Gap from the Historical Event to the Earliest Manuscript Published	36
Table 4	Where the Apostles Operated	48
Table 5	Early Church Fathers and the Texts They Considered	53
Table 6	Gnostic Gospels (for a full expansive list, please see Appendix 6)	59
Table 7	Historical Figures and Their Sources	70
Table 8	The Miracles of Jesus	86
Table 9	Evidence of Sun Darkening	94
Table 10	World Religions and Their Representation	149

I hope you enjoyed reading

HONEST CHRIS†IANITY

For more **content and additional resources,**
or to **book Drew** to speak at your event
please visit: www.honestchristianity.org
or email drew@honestchristianity.org.

If you enjoyed this book,
please consider **writing a review**
with your honest impressions on
Amazon, Goodreads,
or the platform of your choosing.

Thank you in advance, and
please know that your feedback
is highly valued.

**HONEST
CHRIS†IANITY
MEDIA**

www.ingramcontent.com/pod-product-compliance
Lightning Source LLC
Chambersburg PA
CBHW062046290426
44109CB00027B/2750